BABE and the BIG BOYS

BABE *and* the BIG BOYS

One Woman's Story of Breaking Barriers,
Reforming Washington State Elections,
and Living Life Her Way

CATHY PEARSALL-STIPEK

Babe and the Big Boys: One Woman's Story of Breaking Barriers, Reforming Washington State Elections, and Living Life Her Way

www.BabeandtheBigBoys.com

First edition

ISBN: 979-8-9929027-0-9 (Paperback)
ISBN: 979-8-9929027-1-6 (Hardcover)
ISBN: 979-8-9929027-2-3 (eBook)

Library of Congress Control Number: 2025908019

Cover Illustration: David Mowry, funnybookarts@gmail.com
Ghostwriter: Craig Collins
Senior Editor: Amanda Ayers-Barnett, www.ka-writing.com
Cover Design and Interior Formatting: Becky's Graphic Design,® LLC
www.BeckysGraphicDesign.com

Printed in the United States of America

Publisher's Cataloging-in-Publication Data

Names: Pearsall-Stipek, Cathy, author.
Title: Babe and the big boys : one woman's story of breaking barriers , reforming Washington State elections , and living life her way / Cathy Pearsall-Stipek.
Description: Tacoma, WA: Mai Way Publishing, LLC, 2025.
Identifiers: LCCN: 2025908019 | ISBN: 979-8-9929027-1-6 (hardcover) | 979-8-9929027-0-9 (paperback) | 979-8-9929027-2-3 (ebook)
Subjects: LCSH Pearsall-Stipek, Cathy. | Legislators--Washington (State)--Biography. | Legislators--United States--Biography. | Women legislators--United States--Biography. | Civic leaders--Washington (State)--Tacoma--Biography. | Washington (State)--Politics and government--20th century. | BISAC BIOGRAPHY & AUTOBIOGRAPHY / Memoirs | BIOGRAPHY & AUTOBIOGRAPHY / Political | BIOGRAPHY & AUTOBIOGRAPHY / Women
Classification: LCC F895 .P43 2025 | DDC 328.797/092--dc23

Dedicated to my boys, Joe and Rod

Contents

CHAPTER 1

Birth of a Fighter, A Prologue

"**C**ATHY, YOUR SON IS deaf. And you might as well learn to deal with it."

That was the moment. You know how people say your life can change in an instant? Mine changed that day, on April 8, 1964: A doctor—a Big Boy, a certain type of man I'd become more familiar with in the coming years—telling me what my son would or wouldn't do, how my life was going to change, and that I just needed to accept it.

Little did he know. I mean, my God, that doctor had no idea what he started that day, nor the direction my life was going to take. They say God never gives us more than we can handle, but you have to understand that He also has to give us enough to test us, and prepare us for what's to come. And, boy, he sure tested me.

It started on Friday, March 20, 1964, just a normal day with my two little guys: two-year-old Rod and four-and-a-half-year-old Joe. We were off to Dr. Tanbara's office for their yearly check-ups. On that day, I was your typical housewife and mom, and a member of the preschool parent-teacher association (PTA) for our neighborhood school, Arlington Elementary. Life was good:

I had no real worries, was happily married to Ralph, content to watch our family's life unfold in our new house in South Tacoma.

Little did I know, everything would change in just a few short weeks.

Joe's checkup was a little early. Six months earlier, Dr. Tanbara's nurse hadn't been able to get a clear reading on Joe's hearing test. We didn't think much of it. Joe was a busy one, more interesting in playing than sitting still for tests. Dr. Tanbara figured the office might have been a little noisy that day, distracting Joe, so he scheduled a retest with Nurse Diane—Joe seemed to like her, so maybe this time he would cooperate.

While Dr. Tanbara checked on Rod, Diane took Joe into another exam room to give him a test: A machine would give simple instructions at different volumes—Stand up. Pick up the toy—and based on Joe's reactions, they would measure his hearing at different sound levels.

Diane came back with Joe's audiogram, the chart that showed Joe's level of hearing, with a bunch of bars and numbers. I had no idea what I was looking at.

"What does it mean?" I asked Dr. Tanbara.

He studied the chart for a few quiet moments. He seemed surprised, and not in a good way. "It means," he said finally, "that Joe's hearing isn't quite where it should be. It's about thirty percent of normal, in both ears. He has a hearing loss of seventy percent."

Seventy percent? I felt like the world had tilted on its axis. This just didn't make any sense. Joe had been going to nursery school for nearly two years, and his teacher, Mrs. Peg, had never mentioned any hearing problems. He had no trouble interacting with the adults in his life: Mrs. Peg, Dr. Tanbara, Ralph—anyone. He was a gorgeous little guy: blond hair, round face, chubby cheeks, always full of questions. He was bright, happy, and playful, and everyone loved being around him.

Except, now that I thought of it, there might have been some tiny clues. He spoke with a little bit of a lisp—but he was just four years old, right? Nothing to worry about. The only thing that really stood out was how close he liked to sit in front of the TV. He watched most shows without any trouble, but cartoons? They spun him into meltdowns, sometimes to the point of tears. He'd constantly beg to have the volume turned up, which always struck me as so odd. He seemed to hear everything else just fine. So why the earsplitting cartoons?

There was one thing Mrs. Peg had mentioned that totally slipped my mind at the time: Joe sometimes had trouble paying attention in class. There were times he didn't answer when she called his name. But wasn't that something you'd expect of a busy four-year-old?

The audiogram indicated Joe would struggle to hear a conversation at normal volume. Which, clearly, wasn't the case. Even Dr. Tanbara seemed skeptical.

"Tell you what," he said. "Why don't you bring him back tomorrow? It's a Saturday. The office will be quiet. Diane can give him the test again."

I did. Diane said Joe tried hard for her. But the result was the same.

I hadn't mentioned any of this to Ralph, who adored his boys. We'd been told by my physician, early in our marriage, that we wouldn't be able to have children, so when Joe, our first-born, arrived, he was a miracle: beautiful, smart, a little sponge soaking up everything around him. In Ralph's eyes, Joe could do no wrong; he was perfect in every way. I knew Ralph would be crushed to learn anything might be wrong with him. The thought of telling him something wasn't quite right with Joe? It seemed impossible. Even with that audiogram staring me in the face, I still wasn't completely sold on the idea. He was our little guy, functioning like every other kid, both at home and at school. A serious hearing problem? No way.

Dr. Tanbara wasn't quite convinced, either. He wanted a second opinion, so he called an ear, nose, and throat specialist, Dr. Spangler, and made an appointment at his office in the Medical Arts Building downtown.

The boys were frisky that day, wound up like little tops. When we piled into the elevator together, and before I could even tell them which floor we were going to, they were arguing and wrestling over who would push the button. It was classic Joe and Rod, in constant competition for my attention. I did my best to play peacekeeper.

"All right," I said. "How about this: Joe, you push the button that takes us up. And Rod, you'll push the button that will bring us back down. Deal?" They squabbled a bit more, but I was able to negotiate a truce. Joe pushed the button for the sixth floor, Dr. Spangler's office.

Dr. Spangler worked with an audiology expert, someone who knew everything there was to know about hearing tests. We sat together in the waiting room, and of course the boys wouldn't stop roughhousing, arguing over who was going to sit in my lap, when Joe's name was called. I told him to be a good sport and go with the nice lady for another hearing test, and then I watched him walk across the room: a tiny gentleman, quiet and polite as could be. In the midst of all of this, it struck me: He was growing up so fast.

Rod was happy to have me to himself, and he nestled in my lap. We sat quietly and waited for what seemed like forever, though it was probably less than thirty minutes before Dr. Spangler came to the door and called me into the exam room.

The doctor visit routine was familiar by now: One of the boys perched on my lap, the other fussing for attention. Joe didn't like seeing me across the room from him, with Rod, and he let us know it. And over the chatter of the two boys, Dr. Spangler delivered the news, demonstrating a bedside manner that, frankly, left a lot to be desired. He spoke sternly and without any warmth in his voice.

"Mrs. Pearsall," he said, "your son has a serious hearing problem. He won't be going to kindergarten at the public school in the fall. He will never play sports. He will never be able to serve in the armed forces. He will probably never have a normal job."

He listed many other things Joe would never do, but I'd stopped hearing him. His words were like daggers, and the air seemed to have left the room. I felt short of breath. Tears came to my eyes.

"Your son is deaf, Mrs. Pearsall," he said. "And you might as well learn to deal with it."

Dr. Spangler wasn't entirely negative. He was willing to try a few things: surgery to remove Joe's adenoids and, if that didn't work—and he didn't think it would—a hearing aid, which he didn't seem very optimistic about, either. His main recommendation was speech therapy with a specialist at Mary Bridge Children's Hospital, just down the road. But first, surgery, to see if it made any difference for Joe.

I didn't think I was going to be able to drive home, I was so upset. Deaf. I'd never heard such a terrible word. Dr. Spangler had painted a bleak picture of the rest of Joe's life, and who was I to argue? He was the expert. What did I know about deaf children? How would we raise a deaf child?

Nobody had ever spoken to me in the blunt, indifferent tone Dr. Spangler had used. I'd been raised by a loving father who never raised his voice at me, and the men I'd worked with at a local construction company, before Joe was born, were all decent guys. And in Ralph, I'd found a gentle, soft-spoken man. He was a rugged man's man, a City of Tacoma firefighter who hunted, fished, and knew how to do things with his hands: He'd built our entire home on South 76th Street from nothing. He worked a crazy schedule: five days on, two off; then five nights, then three off. On his nights with the other firefighters, he had even learned how to cook. He often had dinner and a drink ready for me when I got home, especially after those late PTA meetings.

This day was no different: I had been thinking, all the way home, about how to break the news to Ralph. Just like Dr. Tanbara, he hadn't been too worried about those first hearing tests. A lot of four-year-old boys talked funny; a lot of them had trouble sitting still and paying attention. To Ralph, Joe was a picture-perfect little boy. And here I was, about to shatter that perfect image.

When we got home, Ralph was ready for us. "There's a drink in the fridge," he said.

It was an ice-cold glass of vodka, and I was happy to have a couple of sips before I sat down and relayed the news. I sent the boys off to play.

"Ralph," I said. "Sit down with me for a second. We need to talk."

He sat and I told him everything Dr. Spangler had told me: Joe's profound hearing deficit, forgetting kindergarten in the fall, finding a new school. I listed all of Dr. Spangler's "nevers," the things Joe wouldn't do, and then mentioned the surgery, the hearing aids.

Ralph just sat, shaking his head. "I don't believe it," he said. "There's nothing wrong with Joe. He's no different from the other kids. He hears me just fine."

That was pretty much everyone's reaction when I gave them the news: our friends and neighbors, our relatives—even

Mrs. Peg couldn't wrap her head around it. Joe played and got along well with all the other kids, she said. The only thing she noticed was that when she spoke to all the kids—story time, especially—Joe liked to be up front, right across from her.

"Dr. Spangler thinks speech therapy could help him do better in class," I said. "He says three sessions each week would do the most good."

This, we both knew, was going to be costly, and we talked about how we might pull it off. More than once, Ralph said again: "I just don't believe this. It's crazy."

Ralph wasn't ready to acknowledge that Joe wouldn't be going to kindergarten with the other kids. It was a tough pill to swallow for both of us. Where would Joe go, then?

⌒⥤⥤⌒

The next few weeks were a whirlwind. Joe's surgery got pushed back because he'd caught a cold, but it finally happened in late May. Just as Dr. Spangler had predicted, it didn't change a thing for Joe's hearing. In the meantime we didn't know what to do, or where to go for help. One night, I was venting about it to a neighbor, Jean, and she told me her husband taught at Birney Elementary, which had a program for deaf students. Birney was practically around the corner, a five-minute drive from our home. It was a new school, built just a couple of years earlier, and I'd had no idea it had a program for deaf kids. Nobody had told me or Ralph about it.

Jean's husband connected me with Mrs. Fisher, the head of the deaf program. She was a nice lady. Mr. Wright, the principal, was also very kind. They explained that they would place Joe with the other deaf children at first, and then figure out the best path forward. It felt like a good fit. Joe hit it off with the other kids, and they were awed by him; he was the only one of them who could talk. When Mrs. Fisher put a set of big, over-the-ear hearing aids on him, his eyes lit up and he looked around the room, trying to pinpoint where all these new sounds were coming from. At recess, while I talked with Mrs. Fisher and Mr. Wright, Joe and his new crew were tearing around the playground on tricycles. He was smiling, happy.

Then came the tough part: telling Mrs. Peg at the nursery school that Joe wouldn't be coming back. She wasn't thrilled about Joe going to a school for the deaf.

"Once he's labeled as 'special,'" she said, "that label is going to stick with him for the rest of his life. I'd be careful about putting him in a class with deaf kids. In my opinion, he is doing fine here."

I assured her that we weren't making any permanent decisions; just doing what we thought was best for Joe.

The Tacoma Public School District had one lone audiologist at the time, a guy named Mr. Zimmer. On Joe's second day at Birney, Mr. Zimmer ran another hearing test and produced yet another audiogram: same story as all the others. With Mrs. Fisher, we decided Joe would begin by spending most of his time with the deaf kids, and over time, as he progressed, he would be integrated into the regular classroom.

And then something happened that Mrs. Fisher probably regretted afterward, but it was a real eye-opener for me: She invited me to stay for a while and watch Joe interact with the other kids.

I will say this about Birney: It has come a long way since 1964. It now has three programs for deaf and hard of hearing students, from preschool up to fifth grade. There's a vibrant community of people, all dedicated to helping to lead these kids toward rich, fulfilling lives. And back then, Birney was kind of a trailblazer. Not many schools had so much as tried to create a program for deaf children.

But what I saw that day? It didn't look like school, at least not in the way I had always understood it. It was more like daycare. At intervals, Mrs. Fisher and her aides tried to teach the kids American Sign Language, and let's just say it didn't seem to be everyone's favorite subject. Some of the kids were really frustrated. But Joe was having a ball. Rod joined him on the tricycles with the other kids at recess and they played games, and Joe seemed to enjoy the ASL session. He had two years of preschool under his belt, and knew how to get along with others. Most of the other kids in the room had been at Birney, in the deaf program, since they were three years old. And as I would soon learn, Joe's ability to speak wasn't the only thing that gave him a leg up on his classmates.

Lunchtime rolled around, and Joe and the other kids his age were plopped into high chairs—I thought Joe was a little old for a high chair, but I held my tongue—and the aides brought them each a dish of food. It looked like a nice little snack. But the boy sitting next to Joe wasn't a fan, apparently. He took one look at the food in front of him and BAM! He swatted his dish onto the floor.

Joe seemed to think that was pretty cool. He'd never seen anything like that, and it probably looked like a lot of fun. He glanced around at the other kids for a moment, and then swatted his food onto the floor. An aide appeared in a flash, cleaned up the mess, whisked the dishes away without a word, and brought the first kid a new dish. He promptly swept it onto the floor again.

I didn't want to scold Joe in front of everyone—that was Mrs. Fisher's job—but I didn't like seeing that, not at all. Joe had never acted like that, at home or at school. He wouldn't have dared. He'd been taught better. I said to Mrs. Fisher: "Please don't bring Joe food again until he's agreed not to launch it across the room."

She said: "Oh, I'm afraid we don't do that here."

I was shocked. Apparently her logic was that a boy who couldn't hear or communicate wouldn't understand why you were trying to correct his behavior; it would only confuse and upset him. That didn't apply to Joe, who communicated just fine. But even if he couldn't? I didn't think such logic should be applied to any child, under any circumstances. If you didn't bother to correct a child who threw his food on the floor, you were teaching him it was okay to throw food on the floor.

This whole food-flinging business really bugged me, and I told Ralph about it that night. He was troubled by it, too, but he seemed to be thinking the kind of thing we'd both been raised to think: We needed to trust the experts. Now, I was starting to have my doubts, but Ralph was willing to accept that this was how deaf kids should be taught. Maybe, he figured, these teachers knew something we didn't. Maybe they had some long-term vision we weren't quite getting.

"Let's wait and see how it plays out," he said.

We didn't have to wait long. We sat down to dinner together, and Joe took one look at his plate and swept it away. It clanged onto the floor and food went everywhere.

Ralph wasn't one to lose his temper, but this really ticked him off. He picked up the plate, salvaged whatever food he could scoop back onto it, and put it back in front of Joe.

"Don't you dare do that again, ever," Ralph said. "You will eat that food now."

Joe burst into tears.

"You can cry all you want," Ralph said, more gently this time, "but you will finish your dinner, and that's that."

After a few minutes of sniffles and shaky bites of food, Joe began to eat like a normal person.

Later, after the boys were settled in bed, Ralph said to me, clearly and firmly: "He's not going back to that school."

✑

So less than a week after we'd moved Joe from Mrs. Peg's class-room to Birney, we moved him back. It was late May, the school year winding down, so there wasn't much fuss about the switch.

Ralph and I turned our focus to Joe's speech therapy, which Dr. Spangler told us he would need three days a week. There was no denying Joe needed help with some sounds: His R's didn't sound quite right, but the S was what really gave him trouble. Ralph and I called S "the million-dollar letter," because that's what it felt like what it cost to send him to Dr. Aden at Mary Bridge three times a week. Ralph had always picked up extra work on his days off: outboard motor repairs at the ma-rina, electrical wiring on new buildings, and odd jobs here and there—but even with that extra income, paying for Joe's speech therapy would be a tight squeeze.

I got a second opinion from Dr. Tanbara, the kind and gentle pediatrician Joe had seen since birth.

"He's never needed any extra attention," I said. "Does he really need all this now? Can his hearing really be that bad?"

Dr. Tanbara couldn't offer easy answers. "I can't tell you what's best for Joe," he said. "You should leave this up to Dr. Aden and Dr. Spangler now. They're the experts." He admitted it was still hard for him to believe Joe had such severe hearing loss. "The way he's adjusted, though, it's probably something he's had since birth," he said. "Not a genetic defect, or anything like that. Probably some kind of nerve damage."

This actually fit a missing piece of the puzzle. During Joe's birth, the obstetrician had lost his heartbeat for a while, long enough that he thought Joe wouldn't make it. Joe came out weak, still covered in the greasy yellow film, vernix, that grows on a baby's skin during the last trimester. He ended up in an incubator for a while, to help his breathing. This was when Dr.

Tanbara had first met Joe: He examined him in the nursery, and told us everything seemed perfectly normal. Everything had always seemed normal with Joe—until now.

Within a few days, Dr. Aden had placed another puzzle piece: Part of Joe's speech therapy would involve learning to read lips. In these early sessions, we learned something that floored us at first, but made sense the more we thought about it: Joe already knew how to lip-read. Apparently, he'd been teaching himself ever since he'd begun to understand spoken language.

This explained a lot: Why Joe sat front and center at story time with Mrs. Peg; why, if his back was to you, he almost never responded to your voice. And cartoons? The characters' lips didn't move like real people's, didn't follow the rules and patterns he'd taught himself.

Here's the thing: Joe's hearing was probably worse than at least some of the other kids at Birney, none of whom could speak. But somehow he had figured this all out by himself. He must have thought this was just how people communicated. He must have thought the world was a really quiet place, where everyone was just learning to get by, like him.

Dr. Aden thought a hearing aid might make Joe an even better lip-reader, and maybe help his speech, if he could hear how other people pronounced the sounds he struggled with. I'll never forget the day she put those things on him for the first time: After the appointment, we were walking down the tunnel that connected Mary Bridge to the main hospital, Tacoma General, and Joe stopped at one of the ashtrays—the pots of sand smokers used to stub out their cigarettes, back when nobody seemed to have a problem with people smoking in hospitals. Joe grabbed a handful of sand, and let it slowly trickle through his fingers. His face lit up, and he looked at me, beaming. He didn't even have to explain: He could hear the whispering noise of the sand falling back into the ashtray. It was probably a sound he'd never heard before.

Our hearing aid excitement was short-lived, though. They helped him pick up more sounds, and made things louder, but the existing technology couldn't quite crack the code of individual syllables. For that, Joe still relied on his lip-reading skills. Over time, he just carried the hearing aids around with him, only using them when he thought they might help. The kid had taught himself lip-reading when he was a toddler, so I knew he would be smart enough to figure out when he needed the hearing aids.

⁓

Luckily, Joe's diagnosis didn't leave me feeling totally lost: Back in the spring of 1959, when I was pregnant with Joe, our neighbor had convinced me to join the preschool PTA group at Arlington Elementary, our neighborhood school. Her thinking? It would be good to know the administrators, teachers, and staff before Joe started there, to learn the ropes and have a say in things. Also, she said, she thought I'd be really good at it.

I didn't think so. I was shy and soft-spoken. I'd never been one to rock the boat. It didn't seem a good fit. But my neighbor wouldn't take no for an answer, so PTA it was. It would turn out to be one of the best decisions I'd made in my life up to that point, especially in the fall of 1964, when Joe was set to start kindergarten. The other parents seemed to like what I had to say, and soon I was elected president of the preschool PTA, which meant I would attend the district's preschool PTA Council meetings. Before long, I knew everyone, all the teachers and administrators not only at Arlington, but across the whole Tacoma Public Schools District. Even the superintendent became someone I was in constant contact with. Like everyone else, I knew him as Mr. B. By the time the next school year began, around Joe's fifth birthday, everyone in the school knew I had a son with hearing problems.

Ralph and I had decided Joe would go to kindergarten at Arlington with all the other neighborhood kids. On the day I took him to register for enrollment, we met the kindergarten teacher who noticed a loop of wire poking out of Joe's front pocket, and asked about it. It was his hearing aid, I explained. She didn't seem to think much of it.

But a few days later, Arlington's principal, Mr. Hanson, called.

"I'm sorry, Cathy," he said. "There seems to have been a mistake. Joe won't be able to attend Arlington this fall. He'll need to go to Birney."

"I've been to Birney," I said. "And there's no way Joe is going back there."

"Cathy. I'm sorry. But Birney is the only option in our district for students like Joe. It's either Birney or Bryant." Bryant Elementary was more than five miles north, west of downtown, near the hospital.

"Listen," I said. "I'm telling you right now, I'm not taking Joe back to Birney. He's going to Arlington. And I'm sorry, but I'm going over your head. I'm calling Mr. B about this tomorrow."

So I did. Didn't even bother calling Mr. B's office or setting up an appointment. I marched right in, stormed into his office, and laid it all out: "Mr. B, Joe is not going to that school. Never again. He's going to Arlington. It's Ralph's and my decision."

This was completely out of character for the woman I had been until that moment. I'd been happy to let the experts, the guys in charge—the Big Boys—call the shots. But no more; no way was I going to let anyone tell me what to do with my son. It was something I would hear many times, in different forms, over the rest of my life and career: *You can't do that* is what it boiled down to. But to hell if I couldn't. I decided right then and there that I wasn't going to listen to these closed-minded, lazy people telling me *I can't*. I can and I will, and I'm going to do it my way.

Two things had fueled this sudden transformation: First, my love, and Ralph's love, for our first-born son, Joe. We knew better than anyone what was best for him, and we weren't going to listen to anyone tell us otherwise. Second, I knew the people who were trying to pigeonhole my son. I'd worked with them, been on friendly terms for more than five years. If I hadn't known Mr. B personally, if I hadn't known I had the backing of other people in the district, there would have been no way I could have barked out orders to the district superintendent.

Mr. B's response was. . . interesting. He took a different approach from Mr. Hanson. I wonder now if he'd learned I didn't respond well to being ordered to do something I didn't want to do. He tried massaging my ego—a tactic I've since learned works well, if you're dealing with other men.

"I know you're upset, Cathy," he said. "I know learning about Joe's disability has been difficult. But we're really proud of what we've built at Birney. You're practically a celebrity in the district now. Everyone respects you. Just think what will happen if they learn you don't support Birney. Your backing would mean the world to our program."

Just like that, Mr. B had become another Big Boy. He was worried about himself, about his district's reputation. And he was trying to play me, to use my popularity as a prod, so that I would do something I knew wasn't in Joe's best interest.

I said: "I don't care what other people think, Mr. B. I'm not doing this. Arlington is his neighborhood school, and that's where he's going."

On a dime, he switched gears. "I'm going to have to change principals, then," he said. "Mr. Hanson has made it clear he doesn't want Joe there." This was ridiculous. Was he trying to scare me? Did he think I cared who the principal was?

It was something I've come to recognize as another tactic straight out of the Big Boy playbook, under the heading: Nice Lady Doesn't Want to Make a Fuss, Now, Does She? He was trying to make it seem as if I would be responsible for some kind of nasty drama the district couldn't afford. This must have worked for him in the past, or he would have known better than to try it with me. He knew I wasn't the meek little mommy who didn't want to stir up trouble or force a principal out of his job. To hell with him! He had another thing coming.

I didn't back down. And I never would, ever again. "Mr. Hanson will just have to get used to the idea," I said. "Whether he likes it or not, Joe's going to Arlington."

And that's exactly what happened. Joe went to Arlington. He got along with everyone, just as he always had. He did just fine.

I was mad for weeks afterward. These Big Boys, these men in their suits, the "experts," had been pushing me and Ralph to lower the bar for Joe, our pride and joy—all so that they could lower the bar for themselves, make their lives easier. They were being thoughtless and lazy—and if there's one thing I can't stand, it's laziness. They wanted us to accept that Joe's life would be what they'd decided it would be: smaller, sadder, with fewer opportunities than the kids they'd decided were "normal." Ralph and I were confused, scared, and clueless about where to even begin. Neither of us had any experience navigating the bureaucratic mess I knew was about to become our daily life.

Thank goodness for the PTA, which had given me some insight into how these "expert" decisions were made. I thought: What about the other people with kids like Joe, who don't have connections, who are being told to do things that might be harmful to their child, and who don't have any way to challenge these so-called authorities?

The meeting with Mr. B had turned me into a completely different person. My life had changed forever. No more of this crap! And I wasn't going to let other families get pushed around by strangers, either.

I was still happy to be a mother and a housewife. But I knew, from that day forward, I would be a fierce fighter for Joe, and for other people who needed a champion. I would not take no for an answer. I would be a leader, not a follower.

For the rest of my life, I would run into them everywhere— the Big Boys—almost all of them men, the ones who were used to calling the shots. I learned how to outsmart and out-maneuver them. I had no idea how many challenges still lay ahead for me and my family—some so tragic they still haunt me; some so dumb I can only laugh at them now—but I knew one thing: They didn't stand a chance.

Deep down, I'm still the quiet, obedient daughter my father had affectionately nicknamed Babe. But let's just say that's not the side most people see. There is nothing that lights a fire like being forced to be a mama bear, and I'm living proof: Once that fire is lit, it never goes out.

CHAPTER 2

Babe

(1932–1952)

IWAS BORN CATHLEEN RAE Emery on April 18, 1932, at St. Joseph's Hospital in Tacoma—but my father called me "Babe" from the start.

Cathy with her father, Wendell

My story really began in 1924, when my grandfather, Samuel Feutz, loaded up a trailer with his family's belongings and moved them all—himself, his wife Maggie, and their five children—from their home near the small farming community of Bloomfield, Indiana, and headed west for Washington State.

Manitou, a neighborhood in southwest Tacoma, was their first stop, before they settled into a house on South 54ᵗʰ Street, the residence that would be their home for years to come. The oldest daughter, Dorothy Cathleen Feutz—Cathleen—had a suitor back in Bloomfield, Wendell Ray Emery, who followed them westward and proposed. Wendell and Cathleen, my parents, were married later that same year. My father established his own business, a used car lot in South Tacoma, to support them. My mother got a job with the Bell Systems Telephone Company.

Obviously, when I was born, my father couldn't have two Cathleens running around. So I was "Babe" and he called my mother "Kack."

I was their only child. Before I was a year old, my parents moved into a little storybook house on North 7ᵗʰ Street, with a white picket fence and a playhouse. With long curls and big blue eyes, I was like a walking doll. Grandparents, aunts, uncles—they all doted on me, couldn't do enough for me.

My mother liked to show me off. Dance classes, beauty pageants—if there was a chance to dress me up and trot me out, she was all over it. She entered me into every dance class and beauty pageant she could find. I was born during the Great Depression, but I never knew what that meant. I never wanted for anything. I lived like royalty in our little kingdom by the park.

Moving from their landlocked Midwestern family farms to Tacoma was a big change for my folks. Tacoma, on the shores of Puget Sound, was practically surrounded by water. They'd never seen anything like it, a sailor's dream, and my parents dove right in. Every free moment found them exploring the Sound on their boat, the thirty-foot Helen B. When they weren't out on the water, they were socializing with friends at the Tacoma Yacht Club. The club, of course, gave my mother another place to put me on display. She decked me out in a bright blue bathing suit, complete with matching slippers and a white-and-blue bathing cap.

My father became a little boat-obsessed. He wanted to build his own—and not just any boat. He was determined to create a masterpiece. So he bought the hull of a fifty-foot yacht and set it up on the vacant lot next door. Every day after work at the car lot, he would tinker away, transforming that bare hull into a work of art: Mahogany paneling inside and a galley equipped with a stove, an icebox, a sink, and a plush green mohair dinette. It was roomy enough for ten people to sleep comfortably.

He finished it when I was five years old, and told me that since he'd named it after me—the *Miss Cathleen*—I would be the one to christen it. This meant I would be smashing a full bottle of champagne over its bow during the big launch ceremony at the Port of Tacoma.

Now, I don't remember much about being five, but not long before the launch of the *Miss Cathleen* there was a short write-up about my father's new boat in the local paper. According to the article, the excitement, or maybe the pressure, of my upcoming responsibility had gotten to me. I had been practicing a little too hard for my big moment. Every glass container I could get my hands on—ketchup bottles, pickle jars, anything I could find—ended up getting smashed against the *Miss Cathleen*'s hull. There was a growing mound of broken glass under the boat. My mother is quoted in the article: "I'm afraid to buy anything from the grocery that comes in a glass jar, for fear she'll take it out and try another practice launching!"

There's a picture with the article: me, perched on a step-ladder next to the giant boat, a real champagne bottle clutched in my hands. Mother had gone all out for the photographer. I'm smiling like a beauty queen, in a white summer dress with matching shoes and a perfect bow in my hair. I have the champagne bottle at the ready.

The big day finally arrived on a bright Sunday morning, perfect for the *Miss Cathleen*'s sendoff. A truck arrived with a giant crane that plucked her right out of the empty lot and gently placed her on a trailer bed. Off they went, the *Miss Cathleen* in her chariot, all the way to the Port of Tacoma. I felt like the most important person in the world that day, with my ceremonial smash of the bottle against her bow.

The Emery's beloved boat,
the Miss Cathleen

Soon after, my father steered the *Miss Cathleen* to her home berth at the yacht club. My parents were absolutely in love with their new floating home—so much, in fact, that within a couple of years, they decided to ditch the house on North 7th entirely, and make the boat their permanent address.

I was seven years old then, a second grade student at Jefferson Elementary School, a four-block walk from our house. The yacht club was way out on the shore of Point Defiance Park, at the northern tip of Tacoma. My parents' decision to live there threw a wrench into my routine. Point Defiance is a beautiful place to visit, but it's not a good jumping-off point for a seven-year-old who needs to get to school: There were no school buses, of course. The nearest city bus stop was at the Point Defiance Zoo, a mile-and-a-half walk from the yacht club.

So for several years I was a weekend and summer resident of the *Miss Cathleen*. Sundays during school weeks meant getting dropped off at my grandparents' place in South Tacoma, where my three rambunctious younger uncles were still living at home. We were together all week: school, homework, playing with the neighborhood kids. I spent hours outside with Delores and Wanda, my two best friends. Then, come Friday afternoons, one or both of my folks would swoop in and whisk me back to the yacht club for the weekend. It was a double life—but I liked both those lives. They suited me.

My grandparents' place in South Tacoma was where my real memories started. I was the apple of my uncles' eyes. My youngest uncle, Dick, was only about five years older than I was, and my grandmother made him take me everywhere with him. He didn't seem to mind that I was practically glued to his side. We rode our bikes around the neighborhood and played with the other kids—kick the can; hide-and-seek—until dinner time or until it started to get dark, whichever came first.

Being a weekender on the *Miss Cathleen* meant there wasn't a lot of time to create close friendships with the kids around the neighborhood. Aside from Delores and Wanda, my best friends were my uncles. While living at my grandparents' home, I attended Edison Elementary School. When I graduated from Edison, it was time to join my folks permanently on the boat, and I enrolled at Mason Junior High in North Tacoma. I was old enough to be my own captain, navigating the walk through Point Defiance Park, all the way to the bus stop near the zoo—and back again, the whole routine in reverse, at the end of the school day. There were no neighborhood kids hanging around the yacht club, no bikes to ride, no games of kick the can. I had moved from kid central to adult central. For the next few years, I would be surrounded by grownups and grownup conversations.

⁓

I was still in elementary school in 1941, when the world went a little sideways: World War II. Rationing. Luckily, my father served on one of the more than 8,000 rationing boards that issued the monthly stamps people could use to buy things like butter, meat, cooking oil, and sugar. I remember we always had enough of these things.

Summers on the *Miss Cathleen* were legendary. My father led me north on magical island-hopping explorations. I was his boy, his first mate, and we were inseparable, spending weeks on the water together. And we burned a lot of gasoline, which was being strictly rationed to keep the war effort rolling.

But my dad was a resourceful skipper. He turned these long summer voyages into trade missions: Many trips we took during those years went as far north as the Strait of Georgia, to the Canadian San Juan Islands. We'd cruise up there with our stash—all the extra butter and sugar we'd managed to save. Canadians had their own rationing system, and they needed butter and sugar as much as Dad needed gas. We brought them sugar and butter that we hid in the bilge, and in exchange they loaded up enough gallons of gasoline to get us back home.

Now, the Strait of Georgia is notoriously cranky: rough seas, nasty weather. One summer we were cruising with another boat, another family on their own trade mission, when their engine sputtered and died. Right in the middle of the strait, mind you: gale-force winds whipping up whitecaps, the *Miss Cathleen* bucking like a rodeo steer.

There was no way my father would leave the other couple. He circled them like a guardian angel while they radioed for help, making sure we'd be there if they took on water—or worse.

It felt like forever before the Coast Guard arrived. I'd never seen my father get nervous about anything on the boat, but he was looking a little shaky. He turned to me.

"Babe," he said, "run down to the galley and grab me a bottle, would you?" He wasn't a drinker—especially not when he was piloting his beloved *Miss Cathleen*—but he looked like his nerves could use some steadying. I guess even our heroes need a little liquid courage sometimes, especially when the sea has decided to torture you and you're the only one around who can keep watch over your friends.

I brought him the booze from the galley. He tipped back a shot, set the bottle down, and went right back to circling the other boat while it tossed about. A while later, as his nerves started to get the better of him again, he took another swig. Finally, after what felt like an eternity, the Coast Guard showed up and towed those stranded souls to safety.

After years of running his car lot, my father had gotten to the point where he could let his manager hold down the fort for weeks at a time. This was how we were able to take our epic summer adventures on the *Miss Cathleen*. One year, Dad and I tackled our longest voyage together: all the way to Ketchikan, Alaska, and back, a round-trip journey of more than 1,200 nautical miles.

It was harder for my mother to get time off from her job at Bell Systems, so while we drove off in the *Miss Cathleen*—her home!—she'd spend those weeks at her parents' house. But she was just as crazy about the water as we were, and she would join us whenever she could: She managed to get away long enough to meet us in Alaska that summer, and join us for the trip home.

One of the highlights of our summers was the annual predicted log races, which weren't really races. Yacht clubs around the Sound would sponsor a competition between captains and crews that would follow an assigned route, usually to Victoria, British Columbia. Each crew would estimate, based on tides, currents, and other factors, when they would arrive at each waypoint—using only a compass, a tachometer; and charts. The winner was the one who came closest to those predicted times.

Living with Mother and Dad full-time on the *Miss Cathleen* made me realize how different their personalities were. My dad couldn't have cared less about our results in the predicted log races. He just loved being out on the boat with us.

Now, Mom? She was super-smart, very intense, a self-taught whiz who hadn't been to college—I don't think Grandpa and Grandma Feutz ever entertained the idea that they would pay tuition for seven kids. My mother worked hard at her phone company job, and always believed in giving time to her community. When she wasn't working, she'd volunteer with the local organization that assisted people who couldn't see. When the war broke out, boom—she was down at Fort Lewis, volunteering as one of the Red Cross's "Gray Ladies," helping the nurses and keeping the patients comfortable.

She was also insanely competitive. When I look back at all those childhood beauty pageants and dance recitals, all the fancy dresses and hairstyles, I can't help but wonder how much of it was really about me. Maybe it was more about her, about her wanting to show off my curls and blue eyes to the world, to make everyone envious of her and her picture-perfect daughter.

The predicted log races? Same story. Just competing wasn't

enough for Mom. She wanted to excel. She enrolled in classes with the Tacoma chapter of the U.S. Power Squadrons, the non-profit that offers classes in areas related to seamanship and navigation. And in no time she had earned qualifications in piloting, advanced piloting, and engine maintenance. She did this mostly to compete in the predicted log races, but she did take a well-deserved vacation once, to charter a friend's 130-foot superyacht on a trip to Alaska.

So she became the sole predictor for the *Miss Cathleen*'s navigation routes in these competitions, and during our races she tore about the deck like a whirling waterspout, flitting from one door to another, checking for landmarks, for snags or rocks or other debris. It was exhausting, watching her. My dad would sit in the wheelhouse, steering the boat, a smile on his face. "Oh, Kack," he would say. "It's okay. Don't worry so much."

From Dad, I learned how to be with people, and especially with the people I loved. He was kind, gentle, and patient. He never raised his voice at me, not once.

Mother set some great examples, too. She showed me how to push and go after things I wanted, how to do more than most people thought possible. When she wanted to get better at piloting a boat, she found out where and how to do it—and then she just did it. As a result, she did something that no other woman in the State of Washington had done: She became a member of the Tacoma Power Squadron, and earned her captain's license.

That being said, she could be a little haughty and standoffish. She was always trying to conquer something nobody else had done before. Her sisters would tease about how, back in the day, when it was time to do chores she would disappear like a squirrel up a tree—literally, climbing into the branches to read a book and let them do all the work. I never saw her show any love or warmth for my father; displays of affection weren't her thing. They had their disagreements—sometimes heated ones—about politics: She was a Democrat and he was a Republican; listening to them filled me with disgust for all things political.

To me, their marriage seemed like another one of my dad's grand adventures: He'd left everything behind to follow Mother to Tacoma. He proposed. She had no plans to do anything else. They were married. That was that.

I grew up as my father's best friend. I didn't feel like my mother was much of a friend at all, until much later in my life.

⌒⊃℮⌒

Twice a year, in the spring and fall, my dad, my mother, and I would take off for a drive back to Indiana to visit his folks. I hated these trips. The purpose wasn't really to visit his folks; it was to buy new cars for the lot and avoid delivery charges. We would start driving early in the morning and wouldn't stop until late at night, and the only stops in between were for bathroom emergencies or filling up on gasoline. I loved my grandparents, but I hated the farm. I'd grown up on a boat. As far as I knew, Bloomfield, Indiana, was just a lot of cows and grass and bugs.

After our short visit, we would drive to Detroit, to either the Ford or the General Motors plant, where my dad would buy three cars right off the line, and then we would drive them home in a caravan: one car tied behind another, connected by a short cable. He drove our car and towed one of the new ones, and my mother drove one and towed one. This was how he added at least six new cars to his inventory every year. And they were, as far as anyone knew, brand new: I can share it now, since Dad has been gone a long time, but he figured out a way to erase those 2,400 or so Detroit-to-Tacoma miles from the odometer. He was a bit of a renegade—but a very sweet and polite one, as renegades go.

⌒⊃℮⌒

In 1947, I landed at Stadium High School, near downtown Tacoma. The campus is a historic landmark. The main building, which looks like a fancy French chateau, was supposed to have been a luxury hotel, but the builders went bust and had to abandon it before it was finished. It's been the setting for two major motion pictures—*I Love You to Death* and *10 Things I Hate About You*—but there wasn't much drama there during my high school years.

My best friend, Bev, was on the cheerleading squad. She was one of the yell gals, and every fall my father would buy a brand-new convertible to deck out in banners and streamers, decorated in school colors, for the football team's pep rallies. He'd cruise around the field while Bev and the crew waved to the crowd. One year, it poured like crazy during the rally, and the paint from the banners bled onto the car, staining it so badly that it wouldn't come off. My dad took it in stride. He laughed it off, got it repainted, and rolled out another shiny new convertible for us the next fall.

My mother pushed hard for me to go to college, to get the formal education she'd never had. It didn't exactly light my fire. School wasn't my strong suit, and I was pretty happy with my easygoing life in Tacoma. But I couldn't really come up with a good argument against going to college, so I applied to the obvious choice—the University of Washington, in Seattle—and was accepted. Back then, the university accepted just about everybody who lived in the state.

In the fall of 1950, I moved to campus, about thirty-five miles north. I joined a sorority on campus, Phi Mu. I was surprised by how much I enjoyed sorority life: It gave me a sense of sisterhood and camaraderie I'd never really felt while hanging out with grownups at the yacht club. It was Marge, my big sister from the sorority, who nicknamed me Cathy. It was the first time anyone had called me that, and I don't know why I hadn't used it years ago. Bev was really my only close companion back in Tacoma, but to get to her from the boat, or to anyone for that matter, was kind of an ordeal.

At the university I was, for the first time in my life, surrounded by people my own age, day and night. I studied home economics and business administration—I think because they seemed like sensible choices. I didn't have much of a passion for either subject, and let's just say I wasn't setting any academic records at UW. I just never really had any interest in a lot of the classes I took—psychology, for example, seemed like a waste of time to me. I didn't see how understanding the human psyche would be of any practical use in the real world, and I couldn't fathom how four years of these kinds of classes would help me.

In the end, I didn't make it to four years. I didn't even last two, but not because I wasn't interested. I wasn't a quitter, and I didn't drop out. Late in my sophomore year, I got a call from my mother. My father was very ill, she said. He'd battled high blood pressure for as long as I could remember, but his symptoms were getting worse now, and his doctors couldn't find a medication or dosage to manage it effectively. There were times when he would lose consciousness. He needed someone by his side, day and night, and with Mom's workload at Bell Systems and all her other commitments, it simply wasn't possible for her to do it.

"I need you to come home, Cathy," she said. And that was that. My college experience was cut short. But I didn't mind, really. There were bigger things at stake.

CHAPTER 3

I Hate Politics

(1952–1956)

MOTHER CALLING ME HOME wasn't a big deal. I missed the boat. Sure, sorority life was fun, but those classes? Dull as hell. And I was happy to help Dad. When I got back to Tacoma, he needed round-the clock attention while his doctors tried to figure out his blood pressure medications. With me around, we could keep it in a range that allowed him to function normally, and not worry about blacking out. At the time, big changes were afoot in medicine, especially in the treatment of high blood pressure, and there were a lot of newly approved drugs popping up, attacking the problem from different angles. Basically, my father's doctors were playing mix-and-match, experimenting, trying to find the magic combination for him.

It had been two years since I'd graduated high school, and most of my friends had gotten married and started their own lives. Some already had little ones. They didn't exactly have time to hang out with their old high school buddy. So, back on the boat, I volunteered to lead a local Girl Scout troop, so I could spend some time away from our berth at the Yacht Club.

While he was completely dependent on me—at least for now—Dad had already begun to think about moving my life beyond his illness, about ways to launch me out of this boat, where I'd lived mostly around adults, into an adulthood of my own. He was a sensitive, empathetic man, and he helped nudge me down the gangplank.

Dad knew a lady who worked for Lou Johnson Inc., a small chain of elite retail stores specializing in women's fine apparel and accessories, and somehow managed to find me a perfect part-time job. There were two stores in the area, and the one where I would work, in downtown Tacoma, was a sight to behold: A dark marble façade over a dozen glassed-in display cases featuring mannequins decked out in Lou Johnson's stylish, upscale evening wear: dresses, wraps and shawls, elbow-length gloves.

I could still keep an eye on Dad, but also get out of the boat and meet other people. I was his medication and blood-pressure manager, with him off and on, but I could work around that schedule. My position wasn't a typical nine-to-five shift: Lou Johnson was all about service, and I was the driver, shuttling clothes to customers' homes so they could try them on in comfort. It was the Lou Johnson way: Buying clothes from such a high-end retailer was a big decision and had to be carefully considered. Customers would try the clothes on in their homes, and if a few days later they'd decided they didn't want them, I would swing by to pick them up.

As my father's doctors figured out the right medications and treatment plan, he started feeling better—so much better, in fact, that I could finally work full-time, and even have a social life. I had met a really fun person named Ethel Shay—Ets, for short—at my doctor's office. She was the receptionist! She was a little older than me and had her own house in University Place. She was a lot of fun, and we really hit it off. Ets had three young kids and I spent a lot of nights at her home with them. Sometimes I'd stay overnight and go to work from there in the morning, which just seemed more efficient than slogging all the way back to the yacht club.

Lou Johnson carried amazing bridal gowns, some of the finest in Tacoma, and part of my job was to manage weddings and bridal showers. For the showers, I would get the gifts all set up, and help the bride get dressed. At weddings, I'd get the bride ready for the ceremony and then for the reception, and after all the festivities were over I would help her change into her honeymoon clothes, pack up the gown carefully, and drop the company car back at the shop.

I racked up the miles driving all over Tacoma. Every morning, I went to pick up the car from the garage and gas station on Broadway, and then I would grab coffee and donuts for the store manager's husband, who was ill, and check to see if he needed anything. After that I would report for duty at the store and start making my rounds. There was a young guy who worked at the garage, Ted Bottiger. I saw him every morning when I picked the car up, and every evening when I dropped it off. Ted was a friendly guy, easy to talk to, and we usually chatted a bit in the mornings and evenings, and when he was filling the car up with gas. After about a week of this routine, he asked me out. It was an easy date, just a few drinks across the street at the Elks Temple, a beautiful old lodge and saloon built when those social clubs were a big deal and had the money to build such things. Ted usually met friends there in the evenings after work.

We dated for a few months. My wedding duties for Lou Johnson involved a lot of standing around, waiting for the bride to need me for something, and I thought bringing Ted along would make them more fun. Ted was good company—but my God, that guy could network. He was no ordinary gas station attendant. At receptions, he'd work the room like a pro, making his way from one rich father or uncle to the next, shaking hands, introducing himself, and charming them for a few minutes before moving on to the next well-dressed gentleman.

My curiosity finally got the better of me, and I asked him

about all the schmoozing and glad-handing. He told me he was laying the groundwork for his political career. He had always wanted to be a state senator, and these weddings? Meeting the heads of families who could afford a bridal gown from Lou Johnson's? They were perfect opportunities to meet potential future campaign donors.

That didn't exactly charm me. All I could think of was my mother and father, their endless arguments about nothing. I'd never wanted to take a side in their political debates; I just wanted them to get along.

"Well," I told Ted. "I hate politics, and I don't want any part of that."

He stopped talking to me about politics, but sometimes when I met him and his friends at the Elks Temple he couldn't help himself after he'd had a couple.

One night, when I was at the Temple with this group, the bartender flagged me down and told me I had a call on the phone behind the bar.

It was Ets. "Cathy," she said. "Listen. I invited a friend over. And he said he was bringing a friend with him. Why don't you come over for a double date?" She wanted me to meet this friend—and she probably didn't want to be by herself with her date and a third wheel.

"Okay. Be there soon," I said. For some reason, I didn't hesitate. I walked out of the bar without even telling Ted I was leaving.

I wasn't expecting to walk in that night and meet the man I would marry in less than a year, but here was Ralph Pearsall: incredibly handsome and rugged looking, a firefighter for the City of Tacoma. The four of us ended up having a fun evening, filled with good conversation, laughs, and shared food and drinks.

There was more to Ralph than his good looks, something I noticed that night: He had a presence. He wasn't a chatty guy;

when he did talk, it was usually in response to someone directly addressing him, and even then, he didn't volunteer much. In fact, I would later learn that his fellow firefighters didn't know we were getting married until about a week before the wedding. Ralph was soft-spoken—he reminded me of my father, in a few ways—but he wasn't dull. When he spoke, people paid attention. I was intrigued by him. And I really liked the way he looked.

I guess the feeling was mutual: He asked if I wanted to see him the following night.

The funny thing is Ted called the next day, wanting to know the same thing. I told him, "Ted, I kind of like this guy I met last night. He's asked me out, too. I think I'll go with him."

Ted said: "Okay." He wasn't a very emotional guy. He was more of a businessman. We still saw each other every morning and evening, for as long as I worked at Lou Johnson, Inc. We got along fine. There were no hard feelings.

As I got to know Ralph better, I began to understand the contrast more completely. I'd enjoyed spending time with Ted, but he could talk your ear off—at the Elks Temple, at wedding receptions, or wherever. He was always explaining something or making his point known, and there were times I just wanted some lighthearted fun. When Ralph wasn't working, he was all about enjoying life, usually out on the water in his fourteen-foot outboard speedboat. When I went with him, his quiet warmth reminded me of the outings I'd had with my dad as a young girl.

Ralph belonged to a group called the Tacoma Outboard Association, or TOA for short. They met at their clubhouse at Titlow Beach, on the city's western shore just south of the Tacoma Narrows Bridge. I remember an evening when Ralph took me out in his boat, to a barbecue at the TOA. The water was pretty choppy that evening, and Ralph's boat didn't have a windshield. Waves kept surging and splashing over the sides, soaking us both, and the people on shore were so afraid for us that some of them came out in a bigger boat to follow us in and make sure we didn't get swamped before we could make it to the TOA ramp.

Ralph's parents were wholesale and retail florists, and owned about half a dozen greenhouses on McKinley Hill. Naturally, they wanted Ralph to get involved in the Pearsall Floral Company like his brother and sisters and several other relatives. But Ralph wanted no part of it. Technically, his parents' place was his permanent residence, but he was hardly ever there. He spent five days on, two days off, and then five nights on and three days off, working for the fire department. In his off-duty hours, he could usually be found doing some odd job, of which he had many, or at a bar somewhere with his friends. Apparently, he had developed something of a reputation as a playboy. But I wasn't worried about it. And I wasn't surprised when, about four months after we'd started dating, he said: "You want to get married?"

Now, I think some women might be put off by a proposal like that; maybe some would think: That's all you got? But I knew Ralph by then. He said only what was necessary. And the flowery speeches and grand gestures weren't necessary. I could tell how Ralph felt from the things he did. I didn't need him to say anything more.

I said: "Yes."

By that time, my mother had gotten wind of Ralph's nighttime habits. "So," she said, "what bar do you think you'll find him at most often?" She was teasing, but I wondered if she might be trying to stir the pot a little.

"I guess we'll find out," I said. I knew why Ralph was doing it. He didn't want to go home to his parents and listen to all the reasons he needed to quit firefighting and join the floral empire. When it was time to come home to me, and to our family, I knew the bars wouldn't be a temptation. And I was right. After we were married, you could set your clock according to when Ralph walked in the door after work.

Jokes aside, my parents and Ralph hit it off from the start. Ralph, the outdoorsman and avid boater, loved taking his little fourteen-foot duck boat out fishing and hunting, so he especially admired the *Miss Cathleen*, which was nearly twenty years old now and in need of TLC. Ralph could fix anything. Electrical, carpentry, plumbing, engine maintenance—you name it, he could do it. Dad was grateful for the help, not to mention the male companionship, and he often let Ralph take the boat out— something I don't remember him ever letting anyone else do, ever. They spent hours together, tinkering on the boat, and they got along well. One day, when the boat was dry-docked for hull repairs, Dad accidentally swung his hammer a little wide, and he split Ralph's finger open. Ralph didn't get upset. He wrapped the finger up and kept working, without a word.

For all the reasons Ralph kept his distance from his parents, he kept me from them, too. I think he thought that once we'd been introduced, his parents would try to convert me to the cause of prying Ralph away from firefighting, toward a quiet life as a florist. Surely, Ralph knew I would never do that. I think he kept me away from them so I wouldn't have to endure the lobbying campaign. After we were married, on special holidays, we would help deliver flowers, and if the furnace needed repairs, Ralph would do it, but otherwise we didn't get involved in the family business.

I didn't meet his mother until about a month before we were married, and let's just say it wasn't a made-for-TV moment. Ralph was away on one of his hunting trips with his best friend, Gene, in Eastern Washington. They did this all the time, and I used to tease Ralph about them, because he and Gene would always take their suits along so that after a long day of hunting, they could dress up and go out to the bar.

So I assumed, when Ralph called me from jail, that one of these fancy outings at the bar had gone off the rails. But apparently, setting out grain as bait to attract pheasants in a farmer's field was against the state law—I could tell Ralph was pretending not to know this, in front of his jailers, but he knew everything there was to know about the state game laws. He needed money to pay the fine, but he wouldn't hear of borrowing it from me—even though we'd be married in a month! This was how strong a buffer he'd built between himself and his parents: He was calling to ask me to ask his mother to wire him the money.

So that was my introduction to my mother-in-law: that time I called to ask her for money over the phone. Nice, right? After I explained the circumstances, she gave me the money, of course, and I went down to the Western Union office and wired it to Ralph.

We were married on November 5, 1954—about five months after Ralph proposed. It was a small ceremony, just us and our families. Ralph's brother Dick stood at his side and Ets was my maid of honor. We didn't want to make a big production out of it—no tuxedo for Ralph, no fancy Lou Johnson gown for me. In fact, I didn't wear a gown at all. We wore simple suits and corsages, all very low-key.

The reception afterward, though? It was an absolute bash. We rented out a hall downtown, and the place was packed—about 150 people, all our family and friends, from the Yacht Club and the TOA. One of the biggest, happiest celebrations I'd ever seen, and it was all for me and Ralph. It made us feel incredibly lucky to have so many loving people in our lives.

Ralph and I moved into our first home together, a second-floor apartment in the McKinley Hill neighborhood where Ralph had grown up. The apartment was near Ralph's parents' home and one of the Pearsall Floral Company greenhouses. It wasn't exactly the Elks Temple—a little rough around the edges—but I thought the apartment was fine. And it had two floors: a living room, kitchen, and bathroom on the bottom floor, and upstairs, our bedroom. The apartment sat directly above a dry cleaner and was next door to Wylie's, a Chinese restaurant that Ralph had frequented a lot before we were married. Before long, Ralph and I called Wylie's our "playroom," because it was usually where we hosted people when they came to visit. I dried our laundry using a clothesline and pulley that stretched over the restaurant parking lot. It worked great, until the line broke and our clothes rained down onto the cars below.

The entrance wasn't exactly grand, either. The door to the apartment was in the alley behind the restaurant; when you entered, you saw two more doors: One led to the apartment, and the other, a glass door, to the dry cleaner. So the nosy gal who owned the cleaner's seemed to know our every move. My patterns were different from Ralph's: As soon as we moved, I left my job at Lou Johnson to work closer to home, at Fuller Paint. Eventually, I landed a position as an inventory clerk at Lundgren Dealers, a local builder's office. I saw the dry cleaning gal every day, going and coming. Sometimes she said hello—but her real purpose in intercepting me was to ask lots of intrusive questions. I mean, she was nosy!

Now, imagine my mother's reaction to this place. Living at a yacht club had colored her expectations. McKinley Hill? Where's that? She'd never been there before, even though it was one of the oldest Tacoma settlements. It's changed quite a bit over the years, but it's always been a working-class neighborhood, as it was then. When Mother first visited the apartment, while Ralph was on a day shift at the fire station, she looked around and said,

"You must really love him, to live here." And that was the first and last time she ever came to the apartment.

You know what? It turned out to be a really fun place to live. But even I had to admit it was a little shabbier than I was used to, so I struck a deal with the landlord: I would give the place a makeover—clean and polish the floors, hang new wallpaper, and generally spiff the place up—if he would knock a bit off the rent. He agreed, and in no time at all, I had transformed the apartment into a warm, cozy haven for me and Ralph.

I knew Ralph was a catch, and I'd heard rumors about other women who thought the same. But when we moved into our first home, I began to understand how big a catch he actually was: He'd been an absolute heartbreaker. He was around my age, but he'd been much busier than I had been in the dating department: At least three of the women in the neighborhood had carried a torch for him—one since childhood! It seemed every woman in the neighborhood had been after him at some point. As a young bachelor, he'd fallen into a pattern: He would date a gal for a while, have some fun, and then end it before things got too serious. He was a regular at Wylie's, and it seemed everyone there knew him on a first-name basis.

The nosy gal was also a little too interested in Ralph. She was one of the snoopiest people I'd ever met. She never spoke plainly, which annoyed me. Instead, she had a way of making comments or asking questions—usually about Ralph—that hinted at what she was thinking. And not long after we moved in, I figured out what she was thinking: She couldn't understand why Ralph would have married me, out of all the women he'd dated. She also seemed to believe I was pregnant. Because why else would he have married me? I found that so irritating—and infuriating—that I began to wear knit clothes, tight around the waist, so nobody could possibly believe it.

Ralph was oblivious to these things. He worked hard, and

when he wasn't working, we were out enjoying ourselves, usually on the boat. We'd upgraded from his little speedboat to a sixteen-foot cabin boat. It was a fast boat, and I became kind of a water-skiing fanatic, taking any chance I could to get out behind the powerful engines and fly over the Sound. We went out on the water almost every week, camping on beaches in the lower Puget Sound. In the summer, we would venture up to Canada, going to Nanaimo, Malibu (no, not that one; the one north of Vancouver), Pender Harbour, and Maple Bay. Sometimes we would meet up with my parents. We became even more involved with the Tacoma Outboard Association, whose members were becoming our closest friends. Those first months of marriage were pure bliss; just happy, easygoing fun.

1955 was a little rougher.

Ralph's best friend at the fire station, Don, lived with his wife Doris and their five kids—each of them under five years old—in a small two-story house in South Tacoma. It was a packed house, to say the least. The four of us hung out all the time. Doris and I hit it off, and I loved being around her little ones. She had her hands full, surrounded by so many babies, and I was happy to pitch in. On the night of her daughter's birthday, I took Doris a cake and ice cream. It was a sweet little birthday celebration, and afterward I went home to our empty apartment. Ralph and Don were on one of their night shifts.

The phone jolted me awake early the next morning. It was Ralph.

"Cathy," he said. "Don and Doris's house caught fire. Four of the babies are dead."

I was shocked. I don't remember how long it took me to ask: "Where's Doris? Can I go see her?"

They were at Doris's mother's house. "Best to leave them alone for now," he said. "They're both pretty shaken up."

Over the next few days, the pieces fell into place: In the center of Don and Doris's house, on the ground floor, was a fireplace. A fire had been burning there during the birthday gathering, and it was still going strong when I left. Sometime during the night, the fire had somehow escaped the firebox, or the chimney, and started burning its way through the house. Doris woke up to the smell of smoke and rushed to the living room, only to find that the phone was on the other side of the flames. There was no way to get to it, no way to call for help, so she bolted outside, desperate to make the call from a neighbor's house.

The door locked behind her. Doris was trapped outside, unable to get back in and get her children out.

When the bell rang to rouse the firefighters from their beds, and the battalion chief announced the address of the fire over the loudspeaker, Ralph was the only one who took notice of the address. Most of the firefighters, unless they were driving, didn't pay much attention to the addresses that came in; they simply climbed onto the rig and rode to the blaze. So when his own address was announced, Don—who was right next to Ralph when the call came in—didn't take any notice.

Ralph kept it under wraps. He knew it would be up to the battalion chief to decide what to do, so he pulled him aside and said quietly, "Chief. That's Don's address." The chief called Don back and broke the news to him, filling him in on the situation. The two of them rode off ahead in the chief's car. It was Don who first saw Doris on the sidewalk, hysterical.

The crew arrived in time to rescue the oldest child, a boy, whom they pulled from a second story window. The other four kids, including the birthday girl, died of smoke inhalation in their ground-floor cribs before the firefighters could rescue them and put out the fire.

It was a nightmare. "Devastating" doesn't begin to describe it. Ralph wouldn't even let me attend the funeral for the children—and honestly, I couldn't argue. I wanted to be there for

Doris and Don, but the thought of seeing all those children, their tiny faces. . . it was just too much to bear.

It was a while before the four of us got together again. They were staying at Doris's mom's place, down on South 76th Street. Back then, the area was practically the countryside: barbed wire fences, horses grazing in the fields. Don and Doris had thrown themselves into finding a new place, anything to distract from their suffocating grief. They'd been given some kind of settlement after the fire, from either the landlord or insurance company—I never asked—and ended up buying the entire block of land, all the fields around their mother's house. Don was going to build a new home for them on one of the lots, he said, right next to Doris's mother.

Ralph perked up. "I've been wanting to build a house for us, too. I've been looking for a good piece of land."

Don said: "Which piece do you want?"

Ralph, ever the gentleman, let me choose. And I picked the lot on the opposite corner, on a hill above the neighborhood, with a view of Mt. Rainier. Ralph wasted no time. He started building almost immediately. Weekends were still ours for fun and adventure, but for the next year, big chunks of his, and my, time off were devoted to building our little dream home on South 76th Street.

CHAPTER 4

Sewing, Scheming, and Securing My Place in Tacoma's PTA

(1957–1962)

FOR OUR NEW HOUSE, Ralph and I chose a smaller floor plan than most couples our age would have gone for. The doctor had told us kids weren't in the picture for us, and we'd taken the news in stride, and decided: Why not build a cozy place on a nice piece of land, on a hill with a view of Mt. Rainier?

Turns out, half of Ralph's firefighter buddies were handymen, each with his own specialty. They were always helping each other out with projects, and Ralph had done his fair share for them. Some were ready to repay the favor, and others were just happy to pitch in. One guy wired the entire house. Another built the cabinets. Another built the fireplace, brick by brick. The only thing I remember Ralph needing outside help with was the roof—something he didn't want to take any chances with. So he went to visit with the carpentry experts at Tacoma's vocational school, Bates Technical College. Those guys were glad to share their expertise with him.

Ralph's dad came by a lot, too. He was always coming and going, delivering flowers or on his way back to the greenhouse.

One day, after Ralph started working on the roof, his dad stopped to say hello, and for some reason decided to climb the ladder and get up on the roof with him. Ralph's fireman/mason friend hadn't finished with the chimney crown yet, and while he was talking to Ralph, his father stepped backward and fell right through the chimney, all the way down to the fire box. Amazingly, he wasn't hurt.

The house Ralph and his friends built has three bedrooms, a living room/dining room, a kitchen, and a bathroom. It's small and lovely, warm and inviting; quiet, like Ralph. I loved it then, and I still love it today, nearly seventy years later. If I have it my way—and I usually do—I'll take my last breath in this house.

I was at work one day, at the builder's office, when my boss came in with some news that had just come over the radio. Back then, radio announcers couldn't resist interrupting everything with news bulletins, sometimes packed with more information than the public needed. This was one of those times, apparently. My boss laid it on me: A fire had broken out at the Tacoma Steam Laundry, the old full-service laundry near Lincoln Park, and one of the firefighters—Ralph Pearsall—had fallen through the roof. The announcer had just broadcast his name over the airwaves, before anyone had the chance to tell me about it.

"Cathy," my boss said, with a concerned look. "You'd better get over there."

I took off, confused, alarmed—panicked, really. I was afraid for Ralph—and afraid to imagine life without him. What had happened? I didn't feel better when I arrived at the scene: It was obvious that the entire building was going to be destroyed. Parts of it were already caving in. I tried to find Ralph—but, dumb me, I couldn't tell one firefighter from another! They were all running around in the same Tacoma Fire jackets, the same helmets and boots. I pulled one of them aside.

"Where's Ralph?" I said.

"He's at the hospital, Cathy."

"Is he okay?"

All he could do was repeat himself: "He's at the hospital. Tacoma General."

So I jumped in the car and took off for the hospital downtown. When I finally found Ralph in his room, I felt a huge relief. He didn't look bad at all: No burns. A few scrapes, maybe. He'd climbed onto the roof to fight the fire with a hose, but the whole thing was ready to crumble, and the roof collapsed underneath him. He fell through and disappeared—for a while, nobody knew where he was. Nobody could get to him. One minute he was there, and then the roof opened up and swallowed him, leaving just his hose behind. Then, after what felt like forever, he stumbled out of one of the doors, smoke billowing around him. Somehow he'd fought his way out of the burning building. The whole laundry burned to the ground within a few hours.

Ralph had messed up his back pretty badly in the fall, and had inhaled some smoke, but he was well enough that nobody at Tacoma General could think of a reason to keep him. They discharged him about an hour after I showed up. His back felt fine within a few days, and he went back to work as if nothing had happened. Not the worst situation he or his crewmates had seen, not even close to it. But about fifteen years later, those few hours in the hospital proved to be an important event in our lives.

☙

It was just months later, early 1959, when Ralph and I got amazing news: Apparently, my doctor had been wrong: I was pregnant! We were ecstatic. We'd been fine with the idea of living out our years together, just the two of us, but now we had a little one on the way, arriving in August.

I remember telling our friends at the Tacoma Outboard

Association, who were some of our closest friends back then; everyone in the TOA loved us. They were practically as excited as we were. They threw us a huge baby shower at the clubhouse, more than 100 people, to celebrate the news and load us up with gifts.

The TOA was pretty much our social life. If it was a weekend, and Ralph wasn't working, we were on the water: I would start getting the boat ready on Friday night, and we would be gone all of Saturday and Sunday, camping and water-skiing and lounging on the beach. The day before Joe was born, in fact, I was water-skiing behind our boat. I couldn't get enough of it. We were often with our core group of TOA friends, six couples, enjoying each other's company. I loved being involved in the TOA, and wanted to be more involved, so I ran for secretary and won.

One of my main jobs as TOA secretary was to make sure the meetings ran smoothly. While the organization brought a lot of joy, like a lot of social groups, it also had its drama. There were some cliques, some personality clashes, some petty history between members, that kind of thing. At one board meeting, we were set to consider a family's application for membership. I didn't know the family well, but other people knew them, and liked them, and were ready to welcome them aboard. Accepting them seemed like a formality.

Except that one of our members—I'll call her Karen— showed up at this board meeting and asked for the floor. "I'm here," she said, "to ask that you not allow my sister to join our organization." I guess some people were aware—I wasn't—that the applicants were Karen's sister's family.

Karen went on and on about why her sister shouldn't be allowed into the TOA, but honestly, I can't remember a single reason she gave. They were junk and nonsense. They made no sense, and they weren't the kind of things any of us could do anything about. It was clearly some kind of family feud that Karen was trying to drag the TOA into. Not my circus.

But I kept my cool. I reminded everyone that none of Karen's objections had anything to do with our membership criteria, which were what we should be focusing on. Karen had some allies on the board, and at first it looked as if the deck had been stacked against her sister's family. But I was able to convince enough of them to switch their votes: In the end, a majority voted to accept their application.

Turns out these people were great additions to the TOA, a lot of fun to have around. Everyone liked them. Even Karen seemed to warm up to them eventually, which made me wonder what all the fuss had been about.

So I started to get a reputation as someone who could get things done and would stand up for people who didn't have allies. My pregnancy had barely begun to show when my neighbor approached me about the PTA. At the time, leadership roles weren't on my radar, but I joined the pre-school PTA anyway. I went to meetings. I took an interest in the things going on at Arlington School. But I wasn't super involved. I had my own life to occupy me: Ralph, work, our pregnancy.

When Joe was born on August 28, 1959, it was a joyous occasion—not only for me and Ralph, but for everyone in the TOA. The youngest kids in the association were already in grade school, and Joe was treated like the TOA's new mascot. On the beach, he was the star: a picture-perfect baby, adorable, chubby, with blond hair and blue eyes, always sporting a sweet smile. The second we showed up at the beach, somebody would be reaching for him, wanting to cuddle and play. There were days I hardly saw the little guy until it was time to pack up and head home.

Winter usually meant less time on the water, but more time cozying up in the clubhouse. Some of the ladies admired the Canadian wool sweaters I'd knitted for Ralph and myself and baby Joe, each with a big boat logo knitted into the pattern. They asked if I would show them how to do it. So every week I taught a knitting class to about a dozen TOA women, and before long everyone in the TOA had a sweater. They were of varying patterns, but the theme had become the unofficial uniform of the Tacoma Outboard Association.

At the time, I made all my own clothes, and some of Joe's, too, so I was known to be quite a seamstress. In one of our knitting sessions, I must have mentioned that I'd redecorated the interior of our first apartment, because one day I got a call from a friend, Irene, who said she wanted to hire me: She and her husband were building a new house, and she wanted me to make all their drapes for them. She had already contracted with a designer, and chosen the fabric. All that was left was to find a draper.

I had quit my job at the builder's office when Joe was born—I was strictly a volunteer, now, in my work with the PTA and TOA—and because Ralph had a good job, we were still doing fine. But I missed the extra money, and I was always on the lookout for ways to earn more—and of course I was always up for a new challenge. I had never worked as a seamstress—for money, I mean—but I'll admit it: I first tried a lot of the things I've learned how to do so I could make a little money.

I told Irene: "Sure! I can do that!"

She said: "Great! I'll have my designer call you and send you the material."

I said: "Sounds great!"

I'd never made a drape before in my life. I had no idea what I was doing. I went to the library, to see if I could find some books that would teach me how to do it, maybe a few simple patterns, but I came up empty-handed.

After a few days I'd started to worry a bit, and I shared my dilemma with Ethel when we were having coffee together.

"Ets," I said. "I told Irene I would make all the drapes for her new house, but I've never done anything like that. I don't know what I'm going to do."

It was my lucky day. Ethel said: "It just so happens that Ruth, my sister-in-law, is in charge of a drapery workroom up in Kirkland. Let me call her and see if she'll help us."

In the meantime, the designer, Helena, had questions. She came to my house for a meeting.

"So, Cathy," she said, "do you use three-inch or four-inch crinoline at the top of the drape?"

I had no idea what she was talking about. I didn't even know what crinoline was.

"Hmm," I said. "That depends on the length. Sometimes I use three, and sometimes I use four." I made a note to ask Ets's sister-in-law about it.

"Okay," she said. "Do you use a double three-inch hem at the bottom, or a double four-inch hem?"

"Well," I said. "That depends on the fabric. Sometimes three, sometimes four."

"Okay. Do you use washable crinoline?"

"Oh, yes," I said. "Always."

"All right," she said. "I'll go ahead and send you the fabric."

A couple of days later, a huge truck pulled up in front of the house. And the driver unloaded what looked like a mountain of fabric; five of the biggest, heaviest bolts I'd ever seen, in five different patterns. I would be making drapes for the living room, dining room, two bedrooms, the kitchen, and the bathroom. I thought, *Oh, shit, Cathy. What have you gotten yourself into?* I called Ethel and told her I was in over my head.

She said: "But you'll get it done. Ruth said we can come up

to her workroom on Sunday. It'll be fun! You'll sew some drapes, we'll have a nice lunch. I can't wait!"

So we drove up together in the station wagon, Ets and I and my five enormous bolts of fabric, and when the sister-in-law, Ruth, saw the fabric, I thought she might have a heart attack.

"This is what you're going to make drapes out of?" she said.

"Well, yeah."

"And you have no idea what you're doing?"

"Well, no."

Ruth said: "Are you crazy?"

"I'm beginning to think so."

She sighed. "Okay," she said. "Come on up."

We followed her up, and she didn't waste any time. She sat me down and said: "You write down everything I say."

The big trick, with drapes—one of the many things I didn't know how to do—is to allow for pleats when you are measuring the panels and planning the spacing of the stitches. "So I'm going to give you a formula," Ruth said. "It's the formula we use here in the workshop."

I wrote down the formula. Ruth was a real taskmaster, putting me through my paces. After a couple of hours, I knew Ets and I wouldn't be having that leisurely lunch. I wasn't going to get a lunch break at all! Ruth wouldn't let me stop. With the formula, I got the pattern and plan I needed to lay out and cut the drapes.

At the end of the day Ruth told me: "Okay, I want you to go home and make all the drapes you can with these sets of numbers. And then come back next Sunday and I'll show you how to make the pleats." This, I learned, was where the crinoline came in: It's the stiff backing fabric that helps pleats keep their shape.

I didn't have a workroom, so I went home and had Ralph set a piece of plywood across the bed so I could lay the material out—an improvement, but it still felt almost impossible; I was hunched over the whole time. I remember draping the first bolt across the bed and staring at it. I had no idea where to start.

"Oh, Cathy," I said. I still say this to myself all the time, when I've gotten myself into something, and I said it to myself a lot as I worked on that first set of drapes—but I finished them, and in the end Irene's house looked gorgeous. I couldn't believe I'd pulled it off. This may sound unbelievable, but I recently visited Irene in that house, and those drapes were still hanging, about seventy years after I'd made them. Still gorgeous. I really outdid myself! I'm still shocked by what I accomplished.

Word got around after Irene had shown them off to a few visitors. Another friend called and said, "Hey, if you're doing drapes, I need some done."

"Sure!" I said. I didn't have any fabric samples to show my friend, so I called Helena, the designer, and asked if she would give me some samples to show.

"Of course," she said. "No problem at all." She brought me some samples of fabric to show my friend, my new client. And after my friend selected the houseful of material she wanted, I ordered it and got to work. This time around, I flew through those drapes, and finished a set that looked just as gorgeous as the first, in much less time. My friend was thrilled, and Helena said: "Wow, these are really nice. Any time you want to sell some more drapes, you go right ahead."

When I gave Helena the bill for the project, I thought she would give me something from the sale of the fabric. But she didn't. Seemed fair, right? I'd done more than simply make the drapes. I'd done the extra work of finding the client and making the sale. I knew Helena charged a markup of about 100 percent on the fabric she used, and I thought I deserved a cut.

She only paid me for my work and nothing for the sale of the fabric. I was pissed.

I decided right then and there that I'd never work under

an arrangement like that again. I applied for a license to do business in the State of Washington—under the name Cathy's Custom Décor—and as soon as it was approved, I got in my car and drove to Seattle to open my own wholesale account to buy fabric. I still considered it a way to make money in my spare time and help keep us in our beautiful house on the hill.

Drapery jobs continued to trickle in here and there, and I still worked with Helena on several projects. There were always new questions:

"Do you know how to make swags?"

"Sure."

"Do you know how to make jabots?"

"Of course."

Hell, I had no idea what those things were, but I figured them out. And soon I was able to move on from making very simple drapes to the fancier ones. I made mistakes—there were plenty of "Oh, Cathy" moments on those jobs—but I was turning into a real pro. I was awfully busy with Ralph and Joe and the PTA, so drape-making was still a part-time, odd-jobs kind of thing, but I enjoyed learning new things, getting better at them, and bringing in a little extra money.

The learning didn't stop with drapes. A group of my TOA friends had decided to take classes at Bates and get certified as Registered Parliamentarians, so that they could help the association's meetings run more smoothly. Among other things, the program taught the basic set of rules—Robert's Rules of Order—that had been used for decades to govern the meetings of groups large and small, from church groups to trade unions. We got our certifications in 1962. Back then, I took those classes because I thought it would be a fun thing to do with friends. Little did I know, what I learned at Bates in those two years would prove useful in the career I didn't even see coming.

Meanwhile, our family had grown again: Rod was born on March 3, 1962. We were prepared for him: I had been using our third bedroom for my drapery business, but in the months leading up to his birth, we converted the attached garage into a big workroom, with its own bathroom. After Rod was born, Ralph built a detached double garage in the back.

Rod was an adorable baby, quiet and calm. When Joe started preschool, I could take Rod with me to PTA meetings. If I had a drapery project, I would hire a babysitter to look after him for a while. There was much more to do, much more to keep track of, but I never felt that God had given me more than I could handle.

That feeling, though, wasn't too far down the road.

CHAPTER 5

Challenging the Status Quo

(1962–1972)

I N THE FALL OF 1964, after everything that had happened in the wake of Joe's diagnosis—the speech therapy, the hearing aids, the arguments with the principal and the superintendent about keeping Joe at Arlington Elementary, our neighborhood public school—I discovered the fight wasn't over: From day one, Joe's kindergarten teacher seemed to resent his presence in class. She complained that because of his hearing impairment, he demanded more of her time—which I knew couldn't possibly be the case. All she had to do was make a few easy tweaks: seating him front and center, or making sure he could see her face when she was talking to him. Just a few simple accommodations that would cost her nothing. But she wouldn't budge. It wasn't about time at all, I think. It was about changing her routine, giving Joe a little extra attention—you know, treating him like an actual person. We had a few meetings about his "behavior," and all she could see were problems. She thought Joe was immature, in need of constant correction. I think the one who needed fixing was her.

Second grade wasn't much better. The teacher had laid down a bizarre, arbitrary rule: No hearing aids allowed. Apparently, reminding Joe to use it was too much trouble for her. It bugged her that he was constantly putting it in and taking it out. For the life of me, I still can't understand her logic. Why wouldn't you want a kid to hear better and learn more?

"If he needs a hearing aid," she said, "he belongs at Birney."

So Joe left his hearing aid at home that year. I think he probably learned as much in second grade as he would have, anyway. I never heard his teacher say much worth listening to, either.

The more frustrated I got with the way Joe's needs were ignored, the more involved I became with the Arlington PTA. Our neighborhood was a mix of folks from all walks of life. A lot of parents were in the PTA, but most worked tough schedules and couldn't always make meetings. Ralph and I weren't exactly getting rich, paying off the house and putting Joe through speech therapy, but at least things were steady—unlike a lot of families at the school. I had time to volunteer, and seeing how many of these parents were struggling to stay aware of, and involved in, their kids' education—well, it worried me. I knew the kids would be the ones to suffer if there wasn't someone fighting for them every day.

A lot of these parents told me they thought I was someone who wouldn't back down from teachers and principals who seemed to have skewed priorities, who wanted to make their own lives easier by making life tough on kids like Joe who needed a little extra help. They saw someone who cared, and when they saw that I was willing to put the effort into supporting them and their kids, they figured I should take on more of a leadership role. So I ran for president of the Arlington Elementary Preschool PTA, and with their support, I won.

Being president meant I automatically had a seat on the Tacoma Public Schools PTA Council, which met regularly to discuss citywide issues.

Remember, this was the mid-1960s. Everything was changing in Tacoma, as it was everywhere in America: The Civil Rights

Act, the Selma-to-Montgomery march, the Voting Rights Act. It felt like there was a new headline every day. Tacoma was as segregated as any other city, and kids from certain neighborhoods were getting a raw deal: far fewer opportunities, much less representation. I worked to get parents involved from every corner of Tacoma, so the district would serve everyone equally. There were some schools where kids didn't even have books. Ridiculous! Why was the district spending more money on some students than others?

The administration, of course, wasn't thrilled with us poking our noses into the business of running schools. Now, they did have some good ideas of their own: To address segregation and take at least a first step toward giving all of Tacoma's kids a fair shot, the district came up with a plan for "magnet" schools. You see magnet schools everywhere today, but it was a brand-new idea then: Set up these amazing schools, with top-notch education and arts programs, in the middle of diverse, lower-income neighborhoods—and in doing so, lure students from white neighborhoods to these areas. It flipped the forced-busing script school districts had been following for years: Instead of shuttling kids from overlooked neighborhoods to white schools, the district was planting its crown jewels in those neighborhoods. It was starting to seem obvious that busing, as a long-term strategy, was only letting schools in under-served areas fall further into neglect and disrepair.

The PTA's disagreements with the administration weren't so much about philosophy, or ideas: We were all really proud that McCarver Elementary School, in the Hilltop neighborhood, wasn't just Tacoma's first magnet school—it was the first in the entire country.

But I've learned that ideas are a dime a dozen. Everyone's got one, but not many people know how to turn ideas into results. Not many people do enough. The magnet school rollout was a perfect example. It was half-assed. One elementary school, one junior high, and one high school? It wasn't enough to move the needle. It felt more like an experiment than a solution. Kids who graduated from McCarver were often stuck going back to the same old routine at their neighborhood junior high. Still, it was a pretty impressive experiment: The teaching and support were so good that I enrolled Joe and Rod at McCarver. They rode the bus for a while, but then I started volunteering at the school, so I just drove them in myself.

I wasn't volunteering so I could keep an eye on the teachers. I wanted to keep an eye on the boys. Hilltop, southwest of downtown Tacoma, was a neighborhood that had been neglected for years. People living there were fed up: It wasn't just that they were being ignored; they were being actively screwed over by the city's new administration. The mayor was trying to kill a federal project that would help rebuild the neighborhood. With the civil rights movement in full swing, these years of frustration boiled over. Protests broke out, and things got ugly, smashed windows and fires everywhere.

One day I was working with the kids in the kindergarten class, and a little girl said to me, very calmly: "My mommy ran out of the house without her clothes on last night. Her boyfriend didn't have time to put on his clothes either."

I was completely lost. "Honey," I said, "what are you talking about?"

"Oh," she said. "Our house burned down." Just another day in Hilltop, I guess.

Ralph worked out of the Hilltop fire station then, and during one of the riots—it may have been the Mother's Day disturbance of 1969, a mess that started after police tried to make an arrest—he and his crew were responding to one of the fires that had been lit. The crowd went wild, trying to yank the firefighters off the side of the rig, and Ralph had to stop and bring everyone inside the cab. Scary times. Let's just say I preferred to have my eyes on the boys during the school day.

∽

You can probably imagine how district officials reacted when I gathered the concerns of as many Tacoma parents as possible and, with their help, sat down and developed a strategic plan, a roadmap for the district to follow in meeting those concerns. The plan had everything: Performance goals, target dates, even ways to measure progress.

The Big Boys of the district did not like this one bit. See, they were used to the PTA being a bunch of ladies who liked to chat and share snacks at evening meetings. We weren't supposed to actually do things, you know? Especially not demand things of them or the teachers. Sure, they preached parent involvement all the time—but not this kind of involvement.

There was a lot we felt needed fixing, things we thought parents should be in the loop about and have a say in. We stuck our noses in everything having to do with our kids' education—anything having to do with school. It could be rewarding, sure, but sometimes it was just frustrating: one round of meetings after another, accomplishing nothing. Change was slow at the local level—administrators and teachers alike weren't exactly jumping at the chance to do things beyond their job descriptions.

I climbed the PTA ladder, to get more things done: president of the citywide Tacoma PTA Council in 1969; president of the Pierce County PTA Council in 1970. But serving in those positions made it clearer to me that any real change for the kids would have to begin at the state level. While I think our district PTA was much more influential when I served, its limits became obvious. As much as we irritated the district bigwigs, we were still the well-meaning ladies' club, looking to feel useful. They were happy to let us think we were making a difference, even if it wasn't nearly enough.

I started paying close attention to some proposed state laws, bills that could address a host of unresolved issues in Tacoma schools. And I thought about other laws that could help students.

One idea, something I had discussed in depth with Joe's speech therapist, Dr. Aden, was this: Every school should be required to have its own audiologist on staff. Kids like Joe would get the support they needed; their issues could be identified and fixed more quickly with regular testing, and a program of teacher training would create friendlier environments for hearing-impaired students. I thought it was a great idea, a game-changer for kids like Joe. But locally? No way. Tacoma schools weren't going to hire audiologists if they didn't have to, and the PTA wasn't powerful enough to set something like this in motion. I began to think about other ways of getting it done.

In the spring of 1969, when I learned I was pregnant again, I thought it was a mixed blessing. In a practical sense, it was a bit of a problem: The boys each had their bedroom, and I'd set up my drapery business in the living room/workroom Ralph had made out of the garage. Cathy's Custom Décor was still a side business, but things got crazy sometimes. During bursts of activity, I would have as many as six friends in there with me, working to finish up a big order.

So we didn't have much space for a new family member, and we had even less time to think about it. Between raising two boys and running a business (which somehow took up less time than my volunteer work as president of the Tacoma PTA Council), I had my hands full. Advocating for parents and tackling issues across seventy-five schools kept me busy. To be honest, I carried that child for months without giving it much thought.

Planning and prepping have always been my superpowers—but this time, I was just swamped.

The closer I got to my due date, the more convinced I was that it was a girl, and I started to get a little more excited about it. No offense to Joe and Rod, but if I was going to have another baby, I thought it would be good to mix things up a little, to have my own Babe to raise. But I still wasn't doing anything to get ready. My mother stepped in and bought a few clothes, so the baby would have something to wear when it was born—I hadn't had any time to make anything myself. Ralph and I finally moved the boys into bunk beds and made the front bedroom for the new one.

Don't get me wrong: A new baby wasn't unwelcome. The idea of a daughter was exciting. It was just a crazy time, with two little guys keeping us on our toes and my head spinning with a million other worries and concerns.

As it turned out, none of those worries would matter. On November 16, 1969, our third child arrived—but he was still-born. The doctor said it was a boy, but I didn't believe him. Deep down I knew it was a girl, and I think he knew how badly I'd wanted it to be. I thought he was trying to soften the blow.

"Let me see," I said.

The room went quiet. I remember one of the nurses wrapping up the baby and taking him away. The doctor gave me a grave look.

"I don't want you to see this baby," he said. "There were some. . . problems. Some deformities. I know this is awful, but maybe it will help to think of it as a blessing. This guy wouldn't have lived an easy life, probably wouldn't have lived very long at all. You have two happy healthy boys. Let's focus on them and move on."

I wasn't ready to move on, not quite yet. When Ralph picked me up at the hospital, we walked out together, down a hallway lined with flowers: Every single one of the seventy-five Tacoma schools had sent me flowers. Outside, I told Ralph to take me to the mortuary across the street, where they'd taken the baby. I didn't want to see the baby—the doctor had convinced me it wasn't a good idea—but I did want to know one thing.

I asked the people at the mortuary if I could see the baby's death certificate. They looked at me like I was nuts, which wasn't exactly new. But they went and got the certificate for me anyway. There, on the line for the baby's sex, was the big letter M.

This may sound strange, but one of the strongest feelings in that moment was a sense of relief—relief that my doctor hadn't lied; relief that I hadn't lost out on the chance to raise my own Babe. Relief that our new little boy wouldn't have to suffer.

Things had been hard enough for our darling Joe. His small difference from kids his age had put him through tons of difficulties—all of them caused by other people. It was never Joe himself causing trouble. I was heartbroken at losing the baby, but I also understood how the world would have treated him. Just as the doctor had said, I felt blessed to have Ralph and two healthy boys, and relieved that our boy's struggles were over before they'd really begun.

So I did what the doctor suggested: I moved on. My family and friends followed my lead. We didn't dwell on it. We all had work to do.

ↄⱥↄ

The limits of the PTA's influence hit me pretty hard in 1971, when I decided to run for the Tacoma Public School Board. It seemed like a good way for me and the parents I represented to have more say in the schools.

Turns out, winning elections takes more than a good reputation as a PTA leader. A seat on the board was still a volunteer position, but it was also an elected office, with a voting population that spanned the entire city. Politics had never been my thing. But winning public office required a completely different set of skills. Running a campaign? Never done it. Fundraising? Not at this scale.

My opponent, Dave Tuell, had citywide name recognition and connections, both on the board and throughout the city: His father had been a member of the Tacoma Public School Board, and the Tuell family ran the Tuell Funeral Home, one of the oldest businesses in town. They seemed to know just about everyone in Tacoma.

Now, I had name familiarity, too, and PTA moms were a powerful voting bloc. But I didn't know the first thing about how to reach voters outside that circle.

Needless to say, I lost the election to Dave Tuell. I didn't even come close. I felt a little stupid afterward, for thinking I could have won without putting together much of a ground game. But, hey, it wasn't the first time I'd tried to do something new without knowing a damn thing about it. I vowed to learn more about campaigning and winning elections.

Sooner than I expected, the opportunity arrived: Just weeks later, I got a call from a staffer in the office of our representative in the Washington State House of Representatives—the 29th district, an area encompassing nearly all of South Tacoma from McKinley Hill to Fort Lewis. Our representative's name? The Honorable Ted Bottiger. He was running for the State Senate for the 2nd District, and wanted me to come work for his campaign.

Ted had been busy since his gas station days, and I'd been well aware of his political career. His name had been in the paper constantly since he'd first been elected to the House in 1964. He was a Democrat, and his positions on schools and education lined up pretty well with ours at the PTA.

Turns out Ted had been keeping tabs on me, too. All my PTA work had kept my name in the news. And while we hadn't talked in years, his memory of me as a friend, along with my reputation as an advocate for kids in schools, led him to think I'd be a great advisor to his campaign on educational issues.

It sounded interesting, so I went for it. I showed up at my first meeting with Ted's campaign committee: very sharp folks, very focused. The campaign was a well-oiled machine, run like a business with a chain of command and different departments working together. They put me in charge of mailings, which I knew nothing about. But I learned fast. I got his campaign literature out to all the registered voters in the 2nd District.

The funny thing was, I did all of this before I'd even met Ted again. I wasn't expecting some grand reunion, where he wrapped his old flame in a sentimental embrace—I don't think Ted had those kinds of relationships. He was an interesting guy, and a Big Boy now. He pushed for policies that would help people, that would bring justice and opportunity to people who lacked them. But his staffers told me he was all business—sometimes even a little cold. He could be funny, they said, but you needed to get at least three drinks into him before he would let his guard down. I remember thinking this, more than once, at the Elks Temple: Ted needed help loosening up.

I do think, when we started dating all those years ago, Ted thought I would be fun to hang out with. But I sometimes wonder if he didn't also see me, Lou Johnson's driver, as a way to connect with the people who had most of Tacoma's money.

So it was really no surprise that Ted never acknowledged me individually after I joined his team—at least not that I can remember. He'd hired me to get a job done, not to reminisce about old times. Frankly, I found this much more flattering.

When I finally saw him for the first time, he stepped into the staff room and started talking to us as a group. I don't re-member whether he even made eye contact with me.

"One of you in this room," he said, "has to run for my

seat." He wanted a candidate who shared his values and positions, he said.

There weren't any takers, but he kept pushing: "We'll help you any way we can," he said. "I think it's the best thing for the people in our district."

Good thing for Ted, he was better at persuading voters in the 29th than he was at swaying his own campaign staffers that day.

But I went home and thought about it. In these few weeks working with him, I'd really begun to learn the ropes, to see the nuts and bolts of a political campaign. I was still a rookie, but I thought that maybe, if I had Ted's team behind me, I had a fighting chance.

So I called Ted. "What would you think," I said, "if I decided to run?"

"Oh," he said. "That would be great! We don't have any women in the legislature."

I said, "Okay then. I'll run."

Once again, I had no idea what I was getting into. This was a completely different ball game. The State House. But Ted talked me through it: How big my staff should be, how many should attend meetings, how to divide up responsibilities, and all that. So I announced my candidacy for the State House not too long after Ted had announced his Senate campaign.

For a while it looked as if I was going to be running unopposed—a Democrat, Ted's protégé. I seemed like a shoo-in. But out of nowhere, here comes this young fellow named Mike Parker—literally, a twenty-five-year-old kid. I don't know where he was from, but he bought a house in South Tacoma and started acting like he'd lived there all his life. Somehow he also got his hands on a big school bus that he painted this weird chartreuse color, and, in dark green paint, stenciled "Vote Mike Parker for the 29th!" on the sides.

Parker was also a Democrat—a Republican wouldn't have much of a chance in our blue-collar district—and he drove that bus to every tavern in South Tacoma, schmoozing with the patrons. He wasn't a newcomer to politics—he'd been a member of the Young Democrats of America, the party's youth wing, for several years. So he not only knew the machinery of elections better than I did, he also knew a lot more people, even before he'd started visiting the taverns. He hired a couple other guys to plant chartreuse and green signs—I guess those were his official colors—in yards on every block in the district.

I'll admit: I was a little blindsided by this friendly fire from another Democrat. It all happened so fast, I really didn't have much time to react. Mike Parker, the young gun, won the seat: To this day, he's still the youngest person ever to serve in the Washington State Legislature.

So clearly, I still had a lot to learn about campaigning. But it would be a while before I had the time: Ted won his Senate race and offered me a spot on his staff at the State Capitol in Olympia. He needed a research analyst: someone to dig into policies, help him write laws, and explain complicated issues and proposed or pending laws to the public. It would mean becoming a commuter, driving a half-hour to Olympia every day and back, and it would force me and Ralph to find an afternoon babysitter for the boys when he worked day shifts. But it was too good an opportunity to pass up. I was ready to learn how things got done at the state level—and I was ready to have a steady, paying job.

One of the first big issues I worked on was a proposed constitutional amendment to authorize a personal income tax. I put together a booklet for Ted and his crew, breaking down the short- and long-term implications. We traveled around the state, hosting workshops to let people know what the proposed amendment would mean. They weren't fans of the idea. To this date, the people of Washington State, and their elected officials, have rejected the idea of a state income tax.

Another big part of my job was helping constituents with their problems: When they came to Ted's office with a complaint, I would research the laws and regulations that applied and write reports for Ted's staff that would guide not only their handling of the issue but how they should communicate that work to the people they represented. Education, of course, was still my pet issue.

I was starting to realize that this whole government thing was much more interesting, and much more important, than I'd ever thought it would be back when Ted had first mentioned his Senate dreams. Who knew? Ted wasn't just all talk. He actually wanted to make things better for the people in his district. And I liked being a part of that.

But this whole period—losing the school board election, getting beat by Mike Parker, going to work in Olympia for a politician, of all things—flew by in a blur. Things were happening fast. And my world was about to be shaken to its core.

CHAPTER 6

Death, Disease, Fever, and Faith

(1973)

RALPH DIDN'T COMPLAIN, EVER. He was a private man. If something was bothering him, you'd never know it. He'd make sure of that. He would do anything for other people—but he never wanted anybody doing anything for him. If he was sick, or feeling poorly, he would keep it from you as long as possible, and then he didn't want to talk much about it.

Which is why this one afternoon sticks in my memory so clearly. Ralph and I had picked out a few ornamental crab apple trees to plant down the side road, and on his day off, while the boys were at school, I got everything together and started digging. Ralph was up, watching television on the couch, and I assumed he would join me any moment. But I got one of the trees planted, and he still hadn't appeared. I didn't care—I could plant trees by myself—but it was completely out of character for him to sit on the couch while I worked at something he could be helping with.

I went in to check on him, and he was still on the couch, watching TV. He looked fine to me.

"Cathy," he said, "I won't be helping you today."

I said that was fine, and I finished planting the trees. But I thought: What the hell is going on?

We found out what was going on just a few months later, in June of 1973. We'd all gathered to celebrate Father's Day on Saturday, a day early, because of Ralph's schedule at the station. It was a sunny day, perfect for sailing. Rod was eleven years old and Joe was almost fourteen, and my father thought they were old enough to learn how to sail. He'd bought them a little sailboat, and planned to take them out on Commencement Bay to show them the ropes.

But when the day arrived, Dad said he wasn't feeling well. So Ralph and I and the boys, and Ralph's brother-in-law, Ed, took the *Miss Cathleen* out onto the bay with the sailboat in tow.

Ralph and Ed had been drinking beer for a while by the time we got out onto the bay. That may have been why Ralph decided he didn't want to go out on the water—but there might have been another reason. He turned to me and said, "Why don't you take the boys out and teach them how to sail?"

So I did. I spent the day with Joe and Rod in the boat—just a tippy little pram, barely big enough to hold the three of us. We got soaked, and they learned the basics. It was a great day on the bay with the boys.

When we met back at the yacht club, Ralph and Ed were still laughing over what had just happened: When Ralph was docking the *Miss Cathleen* into the boathouse—something he'd done many times, gliding right in to berth—he sideswiped both sides of the boathouse entrance.

I laughed, too. "What were you doing?" I said. "You must have had too many beers."

That night, Ralph seemed fine. He got up early the next morning, dressed, and went off to meet one of his fellow firefighters for breakfast at the Flying Boots Café—his usual routine. But less than an hour later, he came home and crawled back into bed.

"Cathy," he said. "When I went to eat I saw three of everything." This was a scary thing to say—and I know he must have been scared—but he said it in the way Ralph usually said things: quietly, matter-of-fact.

At the café, he and his friend Bud had ordered coffee and toast. Everything seemed fine. But after a few minutes, Ralph looked down at the table and saw three cups of coffee, three stacks of toast. He was so disoriented, he couldn't keep it from Bud.

"Ralph," Bud said, "you can't go to the station today. Go home."

So he crawled back in bed when he returned. I didn't bother asking how in the world he'd managed to drive home.

The next morning Dr. Delyanis, a neurologist, asked Ralph some questions and ran a few tests. I don't remember how long we were there, but it seemed like minutes later when Dr. Delyanis sat us down and said:

"I'm sorry to tell you that Ralph has MS."

Ralph and I said, at the same time: "What is that?"

"Multiple sclerosis." Neither one of us had heard of it. Dr. Delyanis explained the basics to us: It's an incurable disease in which a person's own immune system mistakenly attacks the brain and spinal cord, affecting the entire central nervous system. Over time it would degrade the function of other nerves, including the ones that moved Ralph's muscles.

"I can't tell you what it's going to do to Ralph," he said. "It starts differently in everyone, and does different things to different people. The symptoms can be both physical and mental." Ralph's MS had started with his eyes, and for the time being, Dr. Delyanis said, he would focus on that. He fitted Ralph with an eye patch, which would stop his triple vision.

We thought this only meant Ralph wouldn't be working at the fire station for the next few days. We hadn't really taken in what this meant for him, or for our family. We hadn't yet realized that life as we knew it was over.

We decided, since Ralph was going to be off work for a while, to spend some time on the boat together and figure out what we were going to do about all of this. Our friends Frank and Elaine offered to come along, to spend time with us, but also to help with the boat. So we took the *Miss Cathleen* over to Harstine Island, a few passages to the west, and parked the boat in a quiet little cove for a week.

We were a little short on ideas. The future was so uncertain: Would Ralph have times when he was better? If MS was different for everyone, could it turn out that his only symptom would be this problem with his eyes? We could correct that with a patch. We didn't know what to expect, and so we didn't really put together much of a plan. The trip to Harstine Island turned out to be mostly about getting away from home, putting some space between ourselves and the problems we needed to think through.

Not long after our return, before my parents headed off to Indiana for the summer, they sold the *Miss Cathleen*. It had been my namesake, my home, the boat that had carried me away on many adventures with Dad and my mother.

It was another sign that I was living through a time of endings—of losing things. Under normal circumstances, I would have mourned it. But I had no room in my heart. After everything I had been through up to this point, the uncertainty I felt about what lay ahead, I just didn't have the will or the energy to dwell on another loss.

⁓

The problems kept coming. Literally days later—right after we returned from Harstine Island—I discovered a lump in my right breast. I told Ralph about it.

He tried to reassure me—it could be a lot of things, he said, other than cancer. But we both wanted to be sure. "You should see your doctor right away," he said.

I wasted no time. I was at the doctor's office the next day. "We're going to have to do a biopsy on this," he said, "to see what we're dealing with."

Back then, a breast biopsy involved surgery, and a general anesthetic. The next day, when I met my surgeon before the procedure, he didn't say much. I thought he would open up my breast, take a sample from the lump, stitch me back up, and then send the sample to the lab.

What happened was that the anesthesiologist knocked me out, and I woke up without a breast. Nobody had warned me about it, but this was the standard procedure then: As soon as the surgeon had removed a tissue sample, it was sent to the lab for immediate analysis. And if the sample showed signs of cancer, the surgeon would remove the entire breast, while the patient was still asleep. This was how all breast cancer was treated back then, even early-stage cancer.

So I had cancer. But I could hardly think about that or my lost breast. There was so much going on—Ralph's diagnosis, the boys, work, worries about the future—that I mostly felt relieved that this was one problem the surgeon seemed to have solved for me. He stitched me back up and installed a drain tube to keep the wound site clear of any discharge. I would be in the hospital for at least a couple of days, while I recovered and they watched me for signs of infection.

Ralph was doing okay with his eye patch, so he dropped the boys at our neighbor Pat's house—they were still very young, and we didn't want them to see me in the hospital—and came to visit. But before long I got a call from Pat: The boys were very upset, she said. They'd heard the word cancer when Ralph and I were talking about it. So now they knew both their father and mother were sick, and they were scared. She said, "Cathy, I've got to bring them down to see you."

I knew I looked horrible. I called my hairdresser. "Chris," I said. "How fast can you get here? I can't let the boys see me like this."

She dropped everything and came to me, and after she was done, I neatened up and got ready for the boys. I told the nurse, "I need you to let me out of this bed and into the visiting room, because I don't want them to see me in this bed."

Pat brought the boys down, and I sat with them for a while and behaved perfectly normally. I pulled it off: Joe and Rod could see I was going to be okay. And they seemed relieved.

I soon found out the only company that sold prosthetic breasts in those days was Montgomery Ward. You could order one from their catalog. In the meantime, I stuffed Kotex pads into my bra until my two sides matched.

I was ready to put all this behind me: the time I got cancer and the surgeon removed my breast. It might have been the next day that I went back to work at Ted's office in Olympia.

I was still experiencing some pain, still had the drain installed—but I felt the urgent need to get back to work. Ralph's income had been cut in half due to being on leave. We were juggling the house payment, two cars, the RV, TOA dues, and boat maintenance. And it was all on my shoulders now. My life as a volunteer and part-time draper was about to undergo a dramatic shift. I liked working with Ted, meeting new people, and learning about the legislative process. I started to think maybe a career in politics wouldn't be that bad.

⌒∂℮⌒

Later that summer, while I was at work, Sid Snyder, Secretary of the Washington State Senate, flagged me down. He offered condolences about Ralph and my surgery, and told me he had something he wanted me to think about: His wife, Betty, had recently taken the son of a close friend to visit a community of faith healers in the Philippines, and she'd heard about Ralph. She said the healers were doing wonders for the young man. They'd done things for people that couldn't be explained by medical science. People whose doctors had given them months to live went on to live for years after visiting the healers of the Union.

I didn't believe in faith healing. But I owed it to Ralph to at least mention it. His answer surprised me. As soon as I told him about it, he said: "How soon can you get a ticket?"

It shouldn't have been a surprise. Ralph, the strongest and most capable person I knew, had just learned his strength and capability were going to leave him—sometimes slowly, sometimes suddenly. Nothing in his firefighting career—not even falling through the roof of a burning building—had seemed to scare him. I know his diagnosis had scared me. I don't think I realized how frightening it must have been for him.

I contacted the organization, the Union of Christian Spiritists, and found out that a group was leaving the States soon—and that they would gladly welcome Ralph. I booked our tickets for early August.

Our friends and family thought the whole idea was nuts. I asked our neighbor, Tony, if he would lend me his camera so Ralph and I could take pictures on our trip, but he refused. He didn't believe in what we were doing, and he didn't want any part of it. I managed to convince my friend Millie to lend me hers.

We left on the first Saturday in August. My parents had been spending the summer on the farm in Indiana with family, and our neighbor Jay, a lifesaver, generously agreed to drive the boys to Indiana to stay with them—and to bring them back on our return.

Our first stop was in San Francisco, where we met a group of nineteen others seeking cures for their own incurable conditions. We all arrived in Manila about two days later, completely exhausted. We'd had layovers in Hawaii and Guam, and almost no sleep. Our healers, Tony and Marcell, met us at the hotel where we'd be staying in Manila. For two weeks, we powered through the exhaustion, the bad food, the rat-infested hotel, and the strange chanting lectures/prayer services in the hope that something could be done for Ralph. With so much uncertainty, we decided we would focus on getting help for him. If something happened to him—if the "healing" went sideways—I would go home and take care of the boys.

Tony and Marcell worked on Ralph's spine and legs. After a few days Ralph didn't feel so tired—his eyes and his mind both seemed clearer. He mentioned my cancer to Marcell, who insisted on examining me. He looked at the wound site, and my drain tube, and over the next three days performed treatments on my arm and my back—pulling diseased masses of tissue out of me with his bare hands, he said. The mass he pulled out of my arm looked a lot like a chicken liver.

Jay and the boys were waiting for us when we got home. We were—and I am still—full of mixed feelings about the trip. Ralph and I couldn't make any sense of the lectures we'd listened to; like other members of the group, we eventually stopped attending. I'm still not sure I really understand their beliefs.

But I can't say I was completely discouraged by the whole experience. I know a lot of people have a lot of opinions about faith healing, and about this group in particular. And in the long run, while Ralph's MS didn't get better, my cancer didn't get worse—my doctor told me he'd never seen a surgical wound heal so fast, and so cleanly. Some of my friends still can't understand why we took a trip like this, to travel across the Pacific for treatments we knew probably wouldn't help Ralph's condition.

All I can say is that when you're told there's no hope, you'll cling to hope wherever you can find it.

ᥱᷣᥱ

Ralph's vision had cleared a little by the time we returned, and he went back to work for a few days, for the first time in a while. He'd risen through the ranks to lieutenant, responsible for the safety of the crew and coordinating equipment and gear at the scene of an emergency. Everyone welcomed him back, but I think the battalion chief was worried about a possible relapse—the sudden reappearance of triple vision during an incident, for example, could be dangerous. So Ralph was offered a disability retirement.

Ralph felt disappointment, even grief. He'd loved his job as a firefighter. He'd loved being able to help others and support his family. And nearly overnight, all of that had been ripped away.

It was also a financial shock: His retirement pension payments amounted to half his annual salary. Things were about to get rough. But we didn't have much time to think about that, either: About two weeks after our return from the Philippines, I got a call from my mother in Indiana. My father, who was now seventy-two years old, had suffered a heart attack and died suddenly while he was riding his tractor.

By this time, all I could feel was numb. The man who'd nicknamed me Babe and captained our journeys to Canada and Alaska, who'd named his beloved boat after me, was gone.

I was mourning, but I also faced a practical problem: My mother didn't drive anymore, and was stuck in Indiana with the car. Ralph said he was feeling well enough to take the trip with me and help me drive her back. So we went together. There was a quiet, lovely funeral service in Bloomfield, and afterward we drove my mother home.

Days later, Dad's body was brought home to Tacoma, where

his family and friends—dozens of them; everyone who'd met Wendell Emery had loved him—laid him to rest.

ᥱᔛᥱ

I had a couple of months to adjust to the idea of living in a world without my father in it. But 1973 wasn't finished with me yet. In November, a couple of Ralph's friends from the fire station, Frank and Pete, called to let me know they were going on a moose hunting trip, up to Canada. They wanted to know how Ralph was doing, because they were hoping he'd come along as always.

I told them I thought it wasn't the best idea. Since our trip to Indiana, Ralph's MS had gotten worse. There were times when he had trouble walking. He was sometimes incontinent. But ultimately, I said, it was up to them and Ralph.

Ralph wanted to go, and so they did. But they were back within a couple of days. Frank and Pete apologized. It was much harder than they'd expected, they said. Ralph couldn't do much hunting by that point, and I think his friends didn't feel okay about leaving him while they went off to stalk moose.

It was another bitter disappointment for Ralph, a tough pill for all of them to swallow. But worse was yet to come: In a few days—right around Thanksgiving—we would learn Ralph had gotten a urinary tract infection while he was away. He was burning up with a fever, so I took him to the hospital. The doctors and nurses put him in a room with another patient, and asked me a lot of questions about his MS. I felt like they weren't really focusing on the main problem: Ralph had a raging fever.

Ralph didn't get better over the next couple of weeks. The doctors couldn't, or didn't, bring his fever down, and it got so bad that he was delirious, in and out of it for a while. Sometimes he could talk to me, sometimes he couldn't. I went to see him every night. I didn't want to trouble anyone in the neighborhood to watch the boys at the house, so I did the best I could: Every night Ralph was in the hospital, I put the boys to bed, called Pat and told her I was leaving. She kept an eye on the house while I snuck into the hospital after visiting hours and went upstairs to sit with Ralph for a while.

A neighbor, Phyllis, invited Joe and Rod to go along with her family to cut down a Christmas tree. While they were out, the boys, bless their hearts, cut a little tree they brought to Ralph's room and decorated for him. On these nights, in Ralph's room with him, alone behind the curtain, I had the thought, more than once: This tree might end up on his grave. He looked terrible.

One day I got an urgent call from the hospital, asking me to come immediately. There had been an incident with Ralph. His fever had gotten out of control—it had spiked over 106°F, at one point—and he'd started to hallucinate: He was so overheated, he believed he was fighting a fire, and he attempted to "rescue" the patient in the bed next to him—by picking him up and attempting to throw him out the window. The nurses and the orderlies intervened.

When his fever finally broke, we realized the harm that had been done. The high, prolonged temperature had damaged Ralph's brain. He was no longer the Ralph everyone knew. He wasn't always aware of what was going on. He could talk, but he didn't always make sense. He was perfectly pleasant to be around, but he would never be able to take care of himself, let alone hold down a job.

I had a heartbreaking realization: I couldn't take Ralph home. There was no way I could care for him. His disability benefit would cover nursing home care, but not a home health care nurse, and I would have to work to support us and the boys. I was lucky to have my job in Olympia, but even with that, I couldn't afford a full-time nurse.

I didn't have a choice. I hated to do it, but I had to send my Ralph to a nursing home.

Ralph's doctor was kind. He knew we were struggling financially. I'd taken a lot of time off work lately, and with Ralph's reduced income, there were times when I drew my bank account down to a balance of one dollar. I could've used that dollar, but I also needed to keep something in the account so the bank wouldn't close it out. The doctor offered me a shred of hope: If I could prove Ralph's disability was work-related, his payments wouldn't be taxed.

"Was he ever injured on the job?" he asked. "Was he hospitalized for it?"

I told the doctor Ralph was injured, the time he fell through the roof, and he was hospitalized. I went to City Hall, to see if Tacoma might have a record of the fire when Ralph was hospitalized. They didn't.

So I went to the fire station and checked with the battalion chief, who said: "We keep records of everything that's ever happened. They're in the attic."

This was before records could be entered into a computer. The attic was stuffed full of boxes of records, and I crawled around for a while until I found the 1955 boxes. I found the record I needed.

It might seem like a small thing, but it felt like a weight had been lifted, after all that had been piled on over the last seven months.

⌒⌒⌒

Only after all the dust had settled from those months did I begin to understand how these events had taken their toll. It wasn't good. I had fallen into a depression. I remembered the days after I'd learned about Ralph's diagnosis—I was in shock, I think. I reacted by doing something I'd never done: I sat around and did nothing.

From the moment I found the lump in my breast until the day I'd placed Ralph in the nursing home, about ten blocks away from our house, I hadn't had the luxury of inactivity. But now I was home without my husband, responsible for every part of our lives. I worked at Ted's office in Olympia, and relied on my mother for help with the boys. Every evening, after dinner, Joe and Rod and I would go over to the nursing home to see Ralph. The biggest challenge we had was trying to make the visits fun by having something interesting to talk with him about.

These were hard times for me. I just kept telling myself that God never gives us more than we can handle, but I was barely treading water. I didn't feel I was getting anywhere, and I knew I needed to make something happen. God also helps those who help themselves. And big changes were on the horizon.

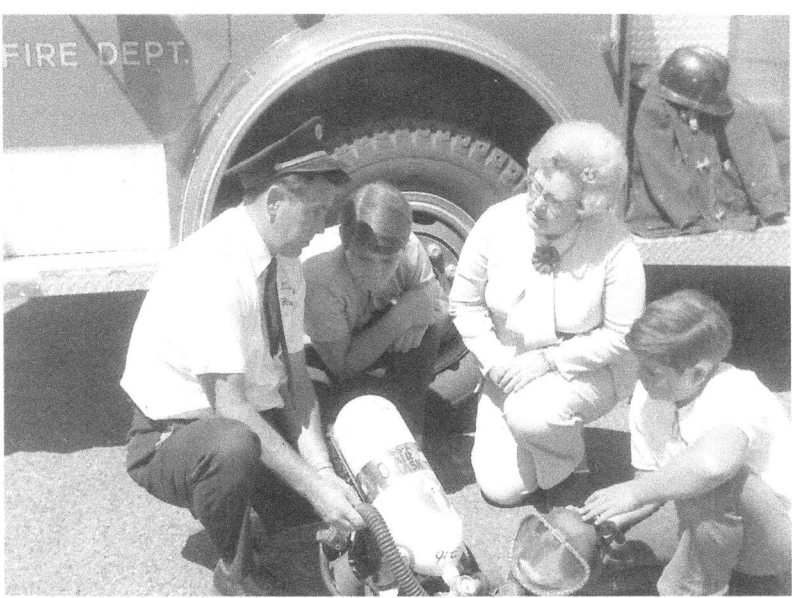

Ralph showing Joe, Cathy, and
Rod fire safety equipment in 1972

CHAPTER 7

Hell, I Could Do This Job Better!

(1974–1975)

BACK IN OLYMPIA AT Senator Bottiger's office, I realized something I'd been missing. I'd been so focused on caring for Ralph by myself that I no longer had a social life. All those friends—the wedding crowd, the boat trips, the knitting classes, Ralph's breakfast and hunting buddies—disappeared when Ralph got sick. In all the time he was sick, I remember three of his friends from the firehouse coming to see him: Pete Grim, Frank Davies, and Clarence Mitchel. I don't remember anyone else. What surprised me most was that nobody from the TOA showed their face. I tried to go to a few club functions by myself, but it just felt weird and uncomfortable. I was the only person there without a partner. Everyone asked about Ralph in a way that felt like they didn't really care about the answer; it was the only thing they could think to ask about now.

I get it: Young people don't like to be around sick people. And I know other people's problems can ruin a good time. And now I know it's only when things go wrong that you learn who your real friends are. Making a clean break from the TOA felt fine. I had to sell the boat anyway.

Volunteering wasn't an option anymore either. With Ralph settled, Olympia offered the only social outlet. Politics, unlike some social circles, didn't require you to be attached at the hip to a partner. And you met interesting people, even though some weren't interesting in a good way.

⁓

After my loss at a run for Ted's seat in the Legislature, Ted asked me to come and work for him in the Senate. I was sitting in the office one day when I heard a booming voice from down the hall. Someone was yelling at the state senator from Kent, Gary Grant—really going off on him, something about a labor issue.

I turned to my coworker, Walt, and said, "Who is that?"

"That's Dave Stipek. The lobbyist for the Joint Council of Teamsters."

"Well," I said, "he's sure got a big mouth."

A few minutes later, in came a very distinguished-looking man, tall, with white hair. As he approached my desk, he announced in a very haughty voice: "I'm the Teamster lobbyist, and I'm here to see Senator Bottiger."

I said, "He's busy right now. But if you want to wait, he'll be with you in a little bit."

"Fine," he said. And he sat down on the edge of my desk, facing away from me. Rude!

"Will you please get off my desk?" I said. "There are chairs over there for you."

He snatched up a newspaper, slumped into a chair, and started reading. After a few seconds he looked up from his paper and again told me, "I'm the lobbyist for the Teamsters, and I need to see Senator Bottiger right away." Pushy!

I thought, *Boy, are you a horse's ass!*

I repeated: "You'll have to wait."

There were only a few women in Washington state politics then. Some had their husbands glued to their sides; others were either single or left their partners at home. Seeing them at events, it started to sink in: I would never have Ralph by my side again. It was a sad reality, but it opened my eyes to a future in politics. It was something I could do, while making a difference for other people, without a public-facing spouse.

In my work for Ted, I stumbled on a discovery that changed everything for our family. A constituent, a firefighter, had asked for help with an issue, and Ted asked me to sit down with the Revised Code of Washington (RCW)—the compiled book of all the permanent laws currently in force in the state—and find all the provisions that related to this person's case.

Buried in a recently passed law, I found a provision that floored me: Apparently, a firefighter on disability re-tirement could have a licensed practical nurse (LPN) care for them at home!

This was huge. When Ralph had moved into the nursing home, our lives were split in two: The boys would get home from school, we'd have dinner, and then I would struggle to get them nursing-home ready. I would say to them: "Okay, now, think of something to say to your dad when you see him." I'm sure they did think of things to say, but once they were there, sitting in Ralph's room, they always clammed up. The staff were kind, but Ralph was so different now. It had to be jarring for the boys to shift out of everyday mode to see their dad in an institution.

I took the RCW into Ted's office and put it on his desk in front of him.

"Does this say what I think it says?" I asked. "Retired fire-men can have LPNs in their homes?"

He looked it over. He said: "I don't remember passing that."

"But is it really what I think it is? I can bring Ralph home?"

"It is," he said. "Take this to the retirement board and tell them you want a nurse at home with Ralph."

The board's reaction wasn't what I expected. They told me no, they weren't going to hire a nurse to care for Ralph at home. They'd never done that, and they weren't going to start. It turned out that nobody had ever used the provision. It had snuck into a law and flown under the radar for several years, and nobody seemed to know it was even on the books.

"Well," I told the board, "I guess I'll just have to bring my attorney down here." I didn't have an attorney, so I decided my attorney was Ted.

He went to the next meeting of the Tacoma Retirement Board, and after a little back and forth, the board realized they were going to have to follow the law. The city hired a nurse, Mary, from a hiring agency, and we brought Ralph home.

Mary would become much more than a nurse to us. She watched over the boys when they got home from school, until I got back from Olympia. She cooked meals. She did laundry. She wasn't just taking care of Ralph—she took care of all of us. It was one of the best things that had happened to our family in a long time.

I was relieved to have Ralph home with us. And the boys seemed overjoyed. No more awkward visits and forced conversations. Joe and Rod just naturally talked to him now, as they joined him for a spin around the neighborhood in his wheelchair, or when they peeked in on him at home. Everything felt a little easier, finally, for all of us. It felt as if our family had been broken, and was getting put back together.

One day at work my boss, Millie Olsen, the Democratic manager for the third floor, came to tell me that Mary had been trying to reach me. Apparently, Joe and Rod had a big blow-up, and Joe had clobbered Rod—and Rod was still on the floor. Mary was afraid he might have been knocked out, and she needed me to come home quickly.

"You'd better go right now," Millie said. "I've called the State Patrol and let them know you're on your way to an emergency." The State Patrol would escort my car home.

Millie had known this news would upset me. "There's a lobbyist out there in the hallway," she said. "I'm going to have him drive you home."

I didn't think that was necessary. "I don't really need anyone to do that," I said.

"But I don't want you driving right now," said Millie. "He's happy to do it."

She was right. I was pretty rattled. All I could think of was Rod, flat on his back. I got my things together and went out in the hallway, and saw that the lobbyist was the Teamsters representative, Dave Stipek, the guy who'd yelled at Senator Grant and sat on my desk. I was so stunned, I didn't know what to say. I didn't want to argue, because there was no time for it. I needed to get out of there and home to Rod. We went down to the lot together, to my car. I was actually glad to have someone with me, as I was more upset than I thought.

Olympia is a half-hour's drive from our home in South Tacoma, and I expected 30 unpleasant minutes with an unpleasant man. But Dave surprised me: He started talking about his family. He was married and his wife, Doris, had a brain tumor that affected her vision and mobility. He also told me he had four children—Alan and his wife, Diane; his daughters Celia, Corinne, and Susan. Then he asked about my family. The entire ride home was spent in family chatter. Honestly, Dave seemed like a decent guy, genuinely curious about other people. A real family man.

Dave and I entered through the back door, and Ralph was sitting in his chair. He looked up when I came in, and said, "You missed all the excitement." It was one of those rare moments when he seemed really present. I missed him terribly in moments like that. There was so much I wished I could talk to him about, ask him about, especially when it came to the boys.

Rod was awake, thank God, when we got home. But his head still hurt, so Dave and I took him to the hospital, where we learned it wasn't that bad. Just a bump and a bruise, but they wanted to keep him overnight for observation.

Dave and I became friends after that day. We'd learned that we had similar home situations and we gave each other strength. To thank him for his help, I hosted him and his family—his wife Doris and daughter Corinne, who prefers to go by Cori—for Easter dinner at our home. Back at work, I was mostly at my desk, but if I saw him in the hallway—which was often; the Teamsters' issues kept him bouncing from one office to another—we'd catch up for a while, mostly about our families. From our conversations, he learned I was considering a future in politics and public service—specifically, I was considering another run at Ted's old House seat in the 29th district.

I ran into Dave at a Democratic Party fundraising event in early December of 1974, and while we were talking, Dean Foster, the Chief Clerk of the Washington State legislature—a good friend of Ted's, and a good friend of mine—approached us.

"Cathy," he said, "we want you to come work for Dave Ceccarelli. We need you."

Since 1967, Dave Ceccarelli had been the Washington State House Representative for the 34th district (West Seattle and Vashon Island). He was a character—a bit of a kook, really, with the attention span of a gnat and the ego of a rock star. He kept a cocktail shaker in his desk, and was always trying to get people—other legislators, lobbyists, staff, even constituents—to try a new drink he'd made up. He was married, but had several girlfriends on the side. Most people found him amusing, but nobody really trusted him. He couldn't remember all the promises he'd made, and follow-through wasn't his strong suit. He rarely showed up to meetings on time, if at all. He always meant to be there, but some shiny object—a funny story or captivating conversation—would catch his interest along the way.

"We need someone to control him," Dean said.

"I don't want to work for that guy," I answered. "I don't even like him."

"You don't have to like him," Dean said. "Think about it."

Dave chimed in. "You know," he said, "it is worth thinking about. Ceccarelli's the chair of both the Banking and the Insurance Committees. A good person to know if you decide to run again. The job itself could raise your profile. And you'll learn a lot."

I thought about it. The lobbyists for those committees wielded big power in Olympia, and Dave was right—they were good people to know if you wanted to run for state office. Plus, someone clearly needed to rein in Representative Ceccarelli. He was a liability to the party, a scandal waiting to happen.

So I told Dean I would do it. In January 1975, the next legislative session, I started work as Representative Ceccarelli's executive secretary. A lot of my women friends, who knew of his reputation, were mad at me for accepting the job. But somebody had to do it, I said. I didn't like him, either. But in politics, you didn't have to like someone to work for them. You just do it.

I answered the phone, handled visitors, wrote all of Representative Ceccarelli's correspondence, did everything that needed to be done. I'll admit, Dave Ceccarelli was fun to be around, cracking jokes and whipping up cocktails for anyone caught in his crosshairs. Something was always going on with him, but it wasn't always something that had anything to do with the job he'd been elected to do.

Dean had told me my most important tasks would be to

make sure Representative Ceccarelli was in his office when he was supposed to be—he liked to go visit his friends—and that he got to his committee meetings. Meanwhile, Representative Ceccarelli told me the most important thing I could do for him was make sure his girlfriends—I think there were four of them—and his wife were never in the office at the same time.

During work hours, I tracked Representative Ceccarelli's movements and kept him on task. I literally walked alongside him, from his office to committee meetings. But he was a wild one, and he needed constant supervision.

The Democratic Speaker of the State House of Representatives, Leonard Sawyer, was halfway through his term when he began to run into trouble with a faction of dissident Democrats who didn't like his style: He had consolidated policy making within his own staff, freezing out Democrats on the legislative committees. So the dissidents orchestrated his ouster, voting him out in 1976. He still had a lot of friends in the House, including Representative Ceccarelli, and they decided to throw Speaker Sawyer a going-away party.

That night, as we were finishing up for the day, Representative Ceccarelli said to me: "Cathy, are you going to the party tonight?"

"I'm going home," I said. "Have fun."

The next morning, on my way to the Capitol, a state trooper pulled me over.

"Follow us," he said. "You're needed immediately."

He didn't explain, but I knew it was Ceccarelli. What in the hell had he done now? I followed the escort to the Capitol, and went straight to Dean Foster's office.

"Cathy," Dean said. "Thank God you're here. Ceccarelli's in the hospital."

"What happened?"

It was a wild story. Apparently the party went late, and

Representative Ceccarelli had decided to go straight from there to work the next morning. The party must have been somewhere on the shore of Capitol Lake, near his apartment, because that's the way he'd driven in, along a road that followed the contour of a steep hill behind the campus. The hill was nearly a cliff, and he'd misjudged one of the turns and plunged down the slope. His car was a crumpled mess. Nobody knew how he'd gotten to the hospital. But the car would be impossible for anyone else to see unless it were brought to their attention. Nobody was that worried about the police showing up at the accident scene before we did.

I asked Dean: "Then how do you know he's in the hospital?"

"He called," Dean sighed. "And he told me he needs you to go down the hill and empty out everything in his back seat before the police get there."

My stomach churned. What was back there? A briefcase full of cash? Bricks of cocaine? A dead sex worker? No way was I going to get tangled up in something like that.

"I won't go," I said, "unless you tell me what's in the car."

Dean was embarrassed. He looked away. "It's. . . some personal items," he said.

"What items?"

He was exasperated now. "Sex equipment," he said.

I laughed and thought: *Why in the hell is this my job? Why don't you go down the hill and clear out the Representative's sex toys?* The only way to the car was on foot, over the cliff, and I was wearing high heels and a business suit.

I arrived at the crash site and had barely made it out of my car when Charlie, the lobbyist for the state's insurance companies, arrived. I don't know how he found out or who called him, but he obviously had an interest in helping the Insurance Committee Chair out of a jam.

"Cathy," he said, "let me help you."

So he and I crawled backwards, like crawdads, down the hill to the car, swept all of Dave Ceccarelli's sex equipment into a bag, and crawled back up the hill. The lobbyist took the bag with him and I didn't ask, or want to know, what he was going to do with it.

I then went to see Representative Ceccarelli at the hospital. He was unscathed. He'd checked himself in as a preemptive measure, hoping to dodge the media storm until things cooled off. He asked me to make sure his girlfriends, wife, and boys didn't visit him in the hospital at the same time.

I dreaded going back to the office. I knew what I was in for. And sure enough, the phone started ringing off the hook, people clamoring for details about the accident, his injuries, whether he would still make it to this meeting or that appointment. I had no answers, and that made a lot of them very unhappy.

And Representative Ceccarelli kept digging a hole for himself, and for me. A couple days later, he disappeared from the hospital like a ghost, leaving everything behind—his wallet, keys, and all his belongings, in the hospital safe. He just vanished.

By now the press had gotten hold of the story, and they joined the ringing chorus of phone calls on my desk. The calls were turning nasty. People were demanding to know where the representative was, and unwilling to believe I had no idea.

After a couple days of this, I marched into the office of the new Speaker, John Bagnariol, who I knew was also a good friend of Representative Ceccarelli.

"I've had it," I said. "What the hell is this? How long do you expect me to keep running interference for this guy? I'm tired of lobbyists and constituents and reporters screaming at me over the phone, calling me a liar. This isn't what I signed up for. Either you tell me where he is—right now!—or I'm quitting, and walking out of here today."

"Okay," John said. "Calm down, Cathy." He told me the

story: Representative Ceccarelli had gone with a few friends, including a few women friends, up to the coastal town of Sequim. He wanted to relax there, soak in the hot tub for a while, let the bad press blow over.

I don't think he was really all that worried about the press. It seemed to me the real solution would have been to face the music and answer questions. Instead, he'd fueled some wild theories with his vanishing act. I think he just really wanted to go to Sequim and soak in a hot tub with some girls, more than he wanted to clear things up.

Back at the office, Dave Stipek, the insurance companies' lobbyist, and the lobbyist for the banking business came each day and helped me with the phone calls and letters. Everyone seemed to want to know what Representative Ceccarelli was up to.

The work seemed unending, and I found myself spending more and more time with Dave and the two other committee gentlemen. Dave and I worked long hours together, and our friendship grew much closer. We found so much in common and so much to talk about—legislature and family. One evening, after working on calls and letters all day, Dave announced that he was going to the Wild Life party and wanted to know if I would like to go. It was a weekly gathering of staff, lobbyists, and members who met to have a few drinks, share some food, talk, and dance—kind of let their hair down. I'd always felt I needed to get home to the boys, so I'd never attended, but this night I decided I would. That same day, one of the other Executive Secretaries for another Representative on our floor dropped by and asked if I was going to the party. She said she wanted to go but didn't have anyone to go with. Dave overheard her, and invited her to join us. Her name was Colleen Anderson, and we agreed that we would meet her there. When we arrived, we were asked to sit with Speaker Bagnariol, a member of his staff, Mary, and the Majority Leader from the Senate, Gordon Walgren, and his staff member, Sharon. Woo, I thought. How did I end up with these big shots? Then Colleen arrived, and as she greeted the Speaker and the Majority Leader, and their dates, she asked each of them: "Is this your wife or your girlfriend?" My jaw dropped, but I soon learned this was just Colleen's way. It wasn't like any party I'd ever been to.

Our legislative session ended *sine die*, with no appointed date to reconvene. On the way out of the building I ran into Dave: "Well, you were right," I said. "I sure did learn a lot."

One of the things I'd learned was that the people who served in the state legislature weren't always Washington's finest. When I looked at someone like Dave Ceccarelli, I couldn't help thinking: Hell, I could serve the people better than that.

So I made that the next thing I would do.

CHAPTER 8

If You Can't Beat Her, Smear Her

(1976–1981)

WHEN RALPH HAD GOTTEN sick—and especially when it became clear he would need round-the-clock care, and that his income would be cut in half—I knew I would have to become strong. But when his father approached me and offered to pay off the balance of our home mortgage, I immediately declined the offer.

"Thank you," I said. "But no thanks. I will do it somehow." He owned a thriving business, and he had the money to take care of it—but no way.

"Well," he said, "don't lose the house."

"I'll make sure I don't."

It was pride, sure. I didn't want anyone pitying us, or even knowing how vulnerable we—Ralph, the boys and me—were. But it was more than that: I couldn't rely on handouts—because the day always comes when help just doesn't arrive. If I wanted to succeed in a political career, to put myself in a position where I could support my family and others like us, I had to be in the driver's seat.

This didn't mean flying solo; politics is a team sport.

Working for Ted Bottiger had been my crash course. I began to understand how the game worked. I dove headfirst into the Democratic party, introduced myself to party leaders, and made it clear I planned another run for statewide office someday. They offered advice, put me in strategic positions—like Ceccarelli's office—where I could learn the ropes, make connections, and make a difference.

So in 1976, when Mike Parker, the 29th District upstart who'd beaten me in '74, announced he was going to run for Congress, I called him and asked for his support in my run to replace him. He was game. I was a good candidate who knew what it took to win a campaign: endorsements from people who mattered, a crack team, and volunteers to help me reach out to voters.

Thanks to my friend Dave Stipek, the Teamsters were already on board. A neighbor hooked me up with her friend, Joan Rutherford, a smart, capable woman who was going through a divorce and looking for something to do.

One of the first things Joan asked me was: "So what are your views?"

I told her: "It doesn't matter what my views are. The important thing is to get elected. Then we can start talking about our views."

Joan was sharp, and I liked her. When she saw the campaign in action at a Seattle fundraiser, she signed on as a volunteer. We clicked, and she became my right hand.

My opponent in the Democratic primary was a local gentleman—we were practically neighbors, living in the same precinct—named Lou Marchesini, a nice guy with a loyal following in the Catholic community of South Tacoma.

By now, I had a lot of friends in Olympia. One of them was a guy I'd met in my PTA days—Dennis was his name—who worked at Western State Hospital just outside Tacoma. Dennis held sway with the state employees' union, and when I told him about my campaign, boom—their endorsement was mine. It was a huge get; several other influential groups followed suit, including the State Labor Council.

Dave wanted to help the campaign because he was my friend, and because he saw his Teamsters' endorsement as an investment he wanted to pay off. He attended meetings, gave good advice, and even hit the pavement with other volunteers, going door to door to introduce me to voters. My campaign volunteers got a boost from South Tacoma youth: Rod and thirteen of his middle-school friends. They were old enough that they wouldn't run wild, and could take a little direction. They were eager to please. Our campaign set up a fund to encourage their participation: Each kid who volunteered to help received $100 to buy clothes for school. We gave them each a Pearsall T-shirt and drove them from one precinct to another, dropping them at one end of a street and picking them up at the other end. They rang doorbells, distributed pamphlets, and generally charmed all the neighbors. The local press ate it up. The kids gave us great publicity.

In 1976, it was still the law in Washington State that whoever filed their notice of candidacy first would be the first name to appear on the ballot. A huge advantage! So Rod rallied his troops to camp out in shifts in the Tacoma County-City Building, right next to the Pierce County Auditor's office. Three at a time, they'd unroll their sleeping bags and hold down the fort until the next shift arrived.

So Pearsall was the first name on the ballot, and we ran a great campaign. We were overjoyed when we won the primary—and exhausted. I couldn't yet imagine campaigning for the general election. I was dreaming of celebrating with Joan at the Pierce County Fair, but we sat down on the couch for a moment—it felt like the first time I'd sat down in a year—and immediately we both fell asleep.

As a Democratic candidate for the legislature, I was invited to a fundraiser at a hotel in Seattle for Jimmy Carter, the Democratic presidential hopeful. I drove to the hotel and made it just in time for the fundraiser. I knew my friend Dave was there, somewhere, but I didn't have much time to talk with him. As I was going through the buffet line, the woman next to me asked about my silver charm bracelet, one of my dearest possessions, loaded with mementos. I'd been collecting charms since I was thirteen years old, when my uncle Dick came home on leave from the service and gave me a bracelet with three little charms on it. After he returned from leave, he was killed at Guadalcanal and is buried in Arlington National Cemetery in Washington, D.C. Since then, I'd collected dozens of charms, and the bracelet had become quite the attention-getter.

I turned to the woman who'd asked. It was Jimmy Carter's wife, Rosalynn! I was taken aback, but she didn't act at all like someone who was jockeying for First Lady. She was warm and soft-spoken, and we got along immediately. Talking with her felt like the most natural thing in the world. She asked me to come up to their room after the fundraiser, so she could spend more time looking at the charms.

This was how I met Jimmy Carter, who was every bit as down-to-earth as his wife. Dave tagged along, and we chatted for a while, about everything but politics. Rosalynn was truly fascinated by my bracelet. We stayed so long with them that when Dave walked me down to my van, the garage had closed. He had to take me home himself, and then drive me back the next day to retrieve the van.

What a night! I loved meeting the Carters, two of the kindest people I've ever met. The experience left a big impression on me. Many years later, as each of my granddaughters grew up,

I gave each her own charm bracelet on her sixteenth birthday. I don't know if any of them will ever get to show theirs off to a president's wife—but you never know.

Cathy wearing both her gold charm bracelet (left side), *and silver charm bracelet* (right side)

The 29th was a shoo-in district for Democrats back then: Winning the primary practically guaranteed a win in the general election. We won easily. My term as the 29th District's representative in the Washington State House of Representatives began on January 10, 1977.

Having worked in the Capitol Building for a couple of years already, I knew it wasn't exactly woman-friendly. When I began my first legislative session, I was one of only seventeen women in the entire House, out of ninety-eight total seats—an improvement over the previous session, but not enough, I guess, for women legislators to merit their own restroom.

The male legislators, the Big Boys, could enter a swanky lounge directly from the House Chamber. They ate and drank and smoked cigars there, and the washrooms had every amenity you could imagine. They even had a dedicated barber who would cut their hair.

The women had nothing. We had to leave the chambers, go down the hall, and use the public restrooms. Thankfully, things have come a long way since then.

My freshman class of legislators was a force to be reckoned with. Several of us went on to do big things in state government. Dennis "Denny" Heck, the 17th District's representative, became Congressman and then Washington's Lieutenant Governor in 2020. Dan Grimm, the 25th District representative, served as State Treasurer from 1989 to 1997 and then Deputy for Pierce County Executive. Myron "Mike" Kreidler became a state senator, a U.S. House representative, and, in 2000, Washington State's Insurance Commissioner, where he's served six terms. Brad Owen, the twenty-six-year-old 24th District representative, later served five terms as Washington's Lieutenant Governor.

After being sworn in, I was selected by the Democratic members to be Secretary of the Democratic Caucus. I had a seat on three committees: Social & Health Services, Energy & Utilities, and Vice Chair of Labor. I offered Joan a job as my secretary in Olympia, but the idea of it made her anxious—so much responsibility. We stayed really good friends, and she volunteered whenever she could.

When I worked for Senator Bottiger and Representative Ceccarelli, I drove to Olympia in the morning and returned home at night. But now that I was a legislator, that wouldn't be possible. Legislators had to be always near the chamber. There were last-minute calls for votes, late-night sessions, unexpected summonses from party leaders. It wouldn't have been possible to leave Olympia at the end of a workday. So I stayed at the Governor House Hotel, near the Capitol, where I shared a room with Representative Phyllis Ericson, and drove home to Ralph and the boys on the weekends.

It was tough, being away from them for long stretches, but we had Mary, and Joe was practically an adult now—seventeen, a responsible high schooler with a job and a girlfriend. Even with his hearing impairment, he'd been an above-average student at every level, and he was incredibly mature for his age. Rod watched over Ralph in the evenings. It was a lot of responsibility for him, at the age of fourteen, but he rose to the job. They were all in good hands—but I still missed them. It wasn't the ideal situation, and I know the boys would've liked me home more, but the bottom line was it was bringing in money, and we needed it.

One of my first priorities as a representative was to bring an issue to the State House that I'd been discussing with Joe's speech therapist, Dr. Aden, for years: the licensing of speech pathologists and audiologists. I consulted with Dr. Aden and other professionals about the provisions, had a bill written to make sure it was worded and formatted correctly, sponsored its introduction, and shepherded it through the Social & Health Services Committee.

The goal of the bill was simple: To make sure that people with hearing or speech impairments received care from true professionals. Every family with a kid like Joe deserved to know what they were getting when they worked with someone who used the title "audiologist" or "speech pathologist." The terms had no real meaning at the time: Anyone could call themselves a speech therapist; nobody had the authority to contradict them. Our bill created a state licensing board and established criteria for licensing. It was a common-sense approach to creating and reinforcing professional standards, and it passed the House and Senate easily—but it was vetoed by our Governor, Dixy Lee Ray. In her veto statement, she wrote that she didn't think a board was necessary.

It wasn't the first time Governor Ray had made me mad, and it wouldn't be the last. She was a brilliant scientist, a PhD, and a former member of the U.S. Atomic Energy Commission. But she was a terrible politician. Decisions came out of nowhere, often with explanations that—if she offered them at all—made no sense, or contradicted something she'd said earlier. And if you crossed her, she held a grudge. I thought her veto was a snap judgment that lacked vision. It completely disregarded the perspectives of people like Joe. The bill was later passed under a governor with some common sense. Today, the Washington Board of Hearing and Speech oversees licensing requirements and professional conduct for hearing aid specialists, audiologists, and speech language pathologists.

In addition to decisions that frustrated me, Governor Ray also made some head-scratching moves. Unbeknownst to me, on top of the three committees I was already on, Governor Dixie Lee Ray had appointed me to be the Migrant Labor Chairman for the State of Washington. I had no idea why she did this. I didn't know anything about farming or migrant labor. Most of Washington's farmlands were on the other side of the Cascade Mountain range, where I almost never visited. I'd spent most of my life traveling by boat on the coast and through the Sound.

But I'd been assigned a job, and was determined to do it as well as I could. I spent many hours driving back and forth over the mountains to Yakima, often in the company of Joan, who didn't want me driving alone. We met with people to learn about the needs of farmers and workers. Housing was the big issue: Because these workers came and went, depending on timings of plantings and harvests, they frequently had nowhere to live. It would be up to the farmers to provide this housing, of course, but they needed money to do it.

It was a long haul from Tacoma to Yakima, and because of the barrier that was the Cascades, there were only two routes from Tacoma: North on Interstate 90 and through Snoqualmie Pass, or south, on State Route 410 through Chinook Pass. While

410 was the most direct route, Dave had warned me not to take it. It was a gorgeous drive, taking you along the east side of Mt. Rainier National Park, winding you through the Cascades, and down through the town of Naches before landing you in Yakima. But it was also a very treacherous drive, particularly through Chinook Pass, which was narrow and curvy, with a rock wall on one side and a steep drop-off on the other. In the winter, Chinook is frequently closed, because of the dangerous conditions. Dave insisted that it was much, much safer to take the northern route, over Snoqualmie Pass, and I promised him I'd stick to it.

After one of these meetings, a farmer invited me to visit his orchards west of Yakima, where he wanted to give me a box of his prize apples. I thought it would be good politics to take him up on the offer, so Joan and I followed him out there, a little west of Naches.

By the time we'd finished visiting with him, it was getting late. It had been a long day, and Joan and I were both tired. Taking the northern route would require us to backtrack more than an hour back to Yakima, so I decided to just keep going on the mountain route.

Big mistake. In one of the high passes, a boulder fell into our path and got wedged between the front tire and the underside of the car. We were literally stuck between a rock and a hard place, and couldn't move the car in any direction. Every time a car passed and the driver asked if we needed help, I gave them one of my cards and asked them to call the State Patrol.

Hours crawled by. It was dark when Joan and I spotted a tow truck coming up the roadway toward us. The driver stopped, got out, and explained that he kept his office at a tavern a few miles down the road, where he'd overheard several people go to the pay phone and call the State Patrol to tell them we were stranded. He knew there wasn't a patrolman within fifty miles, so he'd set out on his own to find us.

"Where you going?" he said.

"Tacoma," I replied.

"Tacoma?"

He towed us all the way home. When Dave found out what we'd done, he was angry that we'd taken such a gamble.

I took the farmers' and workers' concerns to the chair of the House Social & Health Services Committee, A. A. "Doc" Adams, a respected veteran politician who had represented the district next to mine since 1969. He had friends in high places—and not only in the State of Washington. He was tight with our delegation in the U.S. Congress, too.

Representative Adams and I knew getting money from our state budget was a long shot. "I think we should go to D.C.," he said. "Let's see if our folks in Congress can help us score some federal funds for our farmers."

So we went, Representative Adams and his staffer and I, to the District of Columbia. The visit took just a day or two. We met with our congressional delegation and explained the situation. As it turned out, one of our representatives, who sat on the House Ways and Means Committee, knew of a pot of money we could tap. Within forty-eight hours, I had secured the farmers and workers what they needed. And I received a hero's welcome the next time I visited Yakima. I was offered more apples than I could eat in a lifetime!

⁓

Sometime in the middle of our legislative session, I received a phone call, out of the blue, from the office of Congressman Norman Dicks, who represented our neck of the woods—the entire Olympic Peninsula, down to Tacoma—in the U.S. House of Representatives. I don't remember now if it was Congressman Dicks himself who called me, or his aide, Tim Strege. Tim had been one of my supporters a long time ago, until I lost my 1972 campaign against Mike Parker. After that, for some reason, he became an adversary. Interestingly, he was now working as an aide to the congressman.

"Cathy," he said, "how are you planning to vote on SHB 743?"

I was stunned. What was this guy calling me for? A U.S. congressman's office lobbying me on a state bill? I'd never imagined it happening.

SHB 743 was all about limiting the number of oil trans-shipment facilities in the state. It expressly forbid the governor from certifying more than one facility, which would be located west of Port Angeles. The language of the bill suggested that this limitation was due to "environmental concerns," and I knew most of the state legislators, including Senator Ted Bottiger, didn't want any oil tankers in the waters of Puget Sound. Dave Stipek, who was by now my best friend, was all for the bill.

But I smelled a boondoggle. Representative Dicks's office was chummy with the company that planned to build that Port Angeles oil superport: the Northern Tier Pipeline Company, which had formed in 1975 to build a pipeline and bring Alaskan oil to the lower 48. The bill would be a huge gift to the company, basically handing it the entire state of Washington. If passed into law, it would puff up Northern Tier and kneecap its competitors.

I didn't like it. But mostly, I wasn't crazy about the idea of an oil pipeline running through the Green River.

I said I wouldn't vote for it. He tried all the Big Boy tricks on me: Did I really want to be the one to make trouble and get in the way of progress? Did I really want to swim upstream? Wouldn't it be better if I went with the flow? Didn't I want to show my support for the other members of the caucus?

And when none of those tricks worked, he played hardball: "You can't do that, Cathy," he said. "If you don't vote for this, I'll make sure you're never elected to anything, ever again."

I said, as politely as I could, that I couldn't support the

bill. Later, when I told Dave about the call, he was surprised by my opposition, but knew better than to argue. He'd learned I wasn't one to budge.

I found an unlikely ally in Vern Lindskog, a lobbyist for another oil company, Arco. He was fighting a Northern Tier monopoly. And on the day of the vote, he kept checking in with me: "Are you still with me?" he'd say, before dashing off to whip up more votes. He seemed surprised every time I said yes, especially when it became clear that the bill was going to pass—and pretty comfortably. I was one of only twenty House members to vote against it. But I'd stayed true to my beliefs, and I'd kept my word.

Governor Ray vetoed the bill anyway, and Northern Tier never got their pipeline.

◦◦◦

At the end of our long and eventful session, I felt like celebrating our successes and relaxing with the boys. To thank Dave for all his advice and support, I invited him and his family—again Doris, and their young daughter, Cori—to take a trip to Hawaii with me, Joe, and Rod. We all spent a couple weeks together, hanging out on the beach and enjoying each other's company. Ralph, unfortunately, was too sick to join us. He stayed at home, in Mary's care.

And then, before we knew it, it was time to get back to work. I had another campaign to launch, to keep my seat in the House and make good things happen. I would first have to win a Democratic primary: A political newcomer, a former insurance salesman and an Air Force Veteran named Wendell Brown, had decided to throw his hat in the ring.

I wasn't that worried about him at first. Campaigning was in my wheelhouse now, and I had a record of successes, including my win for farmers and migrant laborers. I kept my first campaign's endorsements, and snagged a few more. I had a talented, disciplined, message-focused team with me. And I had the backing of nearly every Democrat in Olympia.

But I would soon find out this would be no ordinary campaign. Wendell Brown was one of the young Democrats in Pierce County who seemed to enjoy stirring things up more than they liked getting things done. He was a buddy of Tim Strege, who seemed to have it in for me.

None of the things that had previously worked in my favor—my experience, my stances on issues, my popularity in Olympia—would matter in this primary election. My staff and I thought everything was going well. In the final weeks of the campaign, I decided to go door-to-door in my South Tacoma neighborhood, reintroducing myself and reminding voters of my record in the House.

Dave Stipek, Cathy, Joe's friend,
Oliver, and Joe barbequing for
a campaign event in 1976

And then one day, things got weird. I stepped onto the porch of a man who, as soon as he saw me, stepped away from the door for a moment, and returned with a baseball bat in one hand.

"Get off my property, you bitch!" he said. "I've heard all about you."

I was so stunned I couldn't speak for a moment. Finally, I said: "What in the world are you talking about?"

"I know what you've been up to. Leaving your sick husband so you can run around Olympia with that other guy."

I still didn't know what he was talking about, but he meant Dave Stipek. It was true that Dave and I spent a lot of time together in Olympia. He was a key supporter and a close friend, and when we were away from Olympia, on the weekends, our families sometimes did things together.

It didn't take long before I learned that Wendell Brown was running one of the dirtiest campaigns the State of Washington had ever seen. As far as I knew, he had no ideas, no platform, no pledges to voters. All he did was run a smear campaign, spreading nasty rumors about me and Dave. At the end of that day, when I got home, one of my neighbors came over. He was excited.

"Cathy!" he said. "You won't believe what that guy Wendell Brown is saying about you. He came to my door and said the most horrible things, about you abandoning Ralph and taking up with another guy. I told him: 'You don't know a damn thing about Cathy. Her sons are my paper boys. Good boys. I've seen her get up in the mornings and drive them on their route around the neighborhood. I've seen her pushing her husband around the neighborhood in his wheelchair.' And I told him to get off my porch!"

But the damage was done. I couldn't wash off the stink. My staffers and I could feel it when we talked to voters: Many were either buying his story, or were at least more interested in the gossip than the real issues. By the fall, it was obvious that, even with my Olympia allies in my corner, my support among voters was fading quickly.

A few days before Election Day, Speaker Bagnariol came by my office to see how things were going.

"I think I'm gonna lose it, John," I said. Wendell Brown had put me in a no-win situation: I couldn't ignore the rumors, because voters wanted reassurance. But denying them would just re-focus people's attention on them. I'd wanted the campaign to be about my record. And Wendell Brown knew he couldn't run against that, so he made the campaign about something else.

Speaker Bagnariol asked: "Do you need more money?"

"Money isn't gonna do it. It's too late."

And it was. I was toast. And apparently, winning wasn't enough for Wendell Brown and his supporters. They needed to taunt me, for some reason. One of his cronies had a device that allowed you to play a recorded laughing sound through a telephone. Every time our home phone rang, it was Wendell Brown and his henchmen mocking us. It was horrible. When you answered, all you would hear was their laughter.

All of this—the smear campaign, the loss, and the taunting afterward—was incredibly upsetting to my son Joe. He was in his senior year of high school now, and both he and Rod had always been intensely involved in my campaigns. And not just in the usual ways, helping to canvass and send fliers and hold my place in line at the Auditor's office; they were both very emotionally invested in the outcomes. I would manage to win more elections than I lost—and when I lost, we were almost always able to learn from it and take it in stride.

But this campaign had been vicious, and I'd never had an opponent cruel enough to mock me after a loss. The laughing telephone calls kept coming, and the night the election results were certified, Joe was so angry and unsettled by them that he got into his car and drove off into a driving rain. The streets were slick, and somewhere in Point Defiance Park he slid off the road, took out a stop sign, and got his car stuck in the mud.

I had no idea where he was, and I got myself really worked up. I called his football coach, Joe Stortini, to see if he could help me find Joe, but he had some people over and wouldn't be available for a while. But he must have made some calls: A little bit later, I heard from Tacoma's new mayor, thirty-year-old Mike Parker. He'd heard about Joe, he said, and he knew I was upset. He wanted to know how I was doing, and told me he'd sent Tacoma police officers out to look for Joe.

It didn't take long for them to find him. It wasn't often you saw a teenage boy walking alone and aimlessly in the rain, down Highway 16 in Tacoma. Mike brought him home himself. The rain seemed to have calmed Joe down some. And the car was just nicked up. No big deal.

But even though I tried not to show it, I was also bitterly disappointed by my loss—and, once I took the time to think about what my loss meant, I was scared.

I had enjoyed my time in the House so much that I hadn't really thought of it as a paying job. But now I felt the weight of that lost income settling on my shoulders. How would I support Ralph and Rod, with Rod still in high school? Joe had just graduated and was working for Boeing now. He had bought a house from my mother and was renting a room to his best friend, Oliver. I felt completely lost. I knew I had a lot to give, and I had tons of ideas for how to make life better for people in my district, especially for those under-served students and parents. But at the time, I didn't think I would ever run for office again. I fell into another depression.

But wallowing wasn't an option. Fortunately, I had other skills. Cathy's Custom Décor had thrived before I'd been a state legislator, and I still had all the equipment tucked away. But this time it was going to have to be more than a part-time endeavor, at least until I found something else to do. The converted garage Ralph had set up wouldn't cut it: I would need more room. I began looking around for a bigger space to lease, a building in South Tacoma to devote entirely to the business. I started advertising, opened another account with the wholesaler in Seattle, and looked for new customers.

Mary, meanwhile, was running into problems of her own. Ralph's muscle control was deteriorating, and she thought he could benefit from some gentle water aerobics; that way he could exercise without the risk of falling or hurting himself. But the local YMCA didn't have any private dressing areas where she could help him.

I said, "Well, we have a big back yard. Why not put in a pool?"

I found a pool contractor, Jim B., who was a nice guy, an honest broker who understood our situation and was willing and able to work within our budget. I mentioned to him I was looking to lease some business space in town, and wondered if he knew of anything suitable for a drapery workroom.

He said, "Why don't you just build a space out back, next to the pool?" His crew would already be on site, with most of the equipment they would need. Constructing the building and the pool together would be a lot cheaper than tackling them separately.

I thought it was a great idea, and I gave him the green light. I told him what I would need for the drapery business, in terms of space—but I also told him to build it more like a pool house, so we could enjoy it after I stopped making drapes. I'd begun to think I might want to return to public service after all.

It turned out to be a lovely building, with an office, a bathroom, a kitchen with a bar, and a big workroom that would make a great entertaining space down the line. I loved it, and

I dove right in. Things were finally looking up: While I ran my business, negotiating deals in the office and making drapes in the workroom, there were days when I could look out the windows and see Mary and Ralph in the pool. I felt happy for the first time since losing the election. Soon the business was booming, enough that I employed three gals to come work for me. It kept me plenty busy, and kept the bills paid.

I kept in touch with my friends in Olympia, too. They didn't like Wendell Brown, and they wanted me back in the legislature. They convinced me to challenge him for his seat in the 1980 election. So I did. But I was reminded that powerful friends weren't the most important factor in an election. The mud Wendell Brown and his coalition of Big Boys had thrown on me was still sticking, in the eyes of enough voters at least. I lost.

This one didn't sting so bad, with everything going on at home. I had other things to worry about, other important decisions brewing. Still, part of me missed working for a cause bigger than my household.

My business continued to flourish. And just when it seemed everything was going well, fate dealt another blow, as if God didn't want me to get too comfortable. In February of 1981, a fire broke out in the pool house and charred a good chunk of the building before firefighters arrived to douse the flames. Later, their investigation determined that the fire had started when the office answering machine had short-circuited.

This was a major hassle, to say the least. Business screeched to a halt, but my friends Cliff and Lynn came to the rescue: They volunteered to let me set up a small workroom in the front room of their home, and I was able to finish the orders we had. I filed a claim with my insurance company, and worked—it was agonizing, how much less I was able to do—while the pool house was rebuilt. Finally, by April, I was able to move back in and pick up the pace. It was a huge relief.

Until October, that is. The weather turned chilly, cold enough that I turned on the furnace for the first time. Suddenly the entire pool house was full of what looked like black tar. It was cinders, residue from the blinds over my desk that had burned and settled into the ductwork below the building, and because so much plastic had burned, it was extremely toxic to breathe. It had been sitting down there for months, waiting to poison the air.

The insurance company had been happy to pay the first claim, but the adjustor let me know I was on my own this time; the company was under no obligation to replace the ductwork. To replace the ductwork—which had been installed below a concrete slab—was going to cost a small fortune. It was outrageous. A faulty answering machine had started the fire. Why was I the one holding the bag?

I called my lawyer. There was no other choice: We had to take the manufacturer of the answering machine, Sears, Roebuck and Co., to court.

This kicked off a months-long back-and-forth with Sears. Their "expert" had the gall to claim I'd been using the machine wrong. It was laughable, but how could I prove otherwise?

One day, while the lawyers argued back and forth, two young men showed up at my door. They were dressed alike, in beige pants and navy jackets, and they told me they were from the bank. They were sorry to tell me that I had missed enough mortgage payments that they were going to have to initiate foreclosure proceedings against me.

"You want this house, you can have it," I said. "But when you try to sell it, you're going to have to disclose that it's loaded with cancer-causing chemicals."

The young men left. I never heard from the bank again.

I did a little homework and found out that the same model of answering machine had started several other fires. It was a built-in defect. All my lawyer had to do was ask the "expert," on cross-examination, if the answering machine had caused other fires, and he was forced to cough up the truth under oath. We won the case, and Sears was found liable for all the necessary work.

Ever since my first loss to Wendell Brown, my life had progressed in this way: One step forward; two steps back. Until the pool house was usable again, I wasn't able to make any drapes. My income nosedived, and then grew again when I was finally able to return to the pool house. For a few months, I was back in business.

CHAPTER 9

A Brazen Woman's Journey from Tacoma's School Board to Pierce County Council

(1981–1989)

IN 1981, OUR SON Joe married his high school sweetheart, Jill, in Tacoma. They lived together in the house he bought from my mother, before building and moving into their own house in northeast Tacoma. In 1983, my first granddaughter, Jamie, was born. Joe stuck with Boeing for a few years, but then got the itch to be his own boss, just like his grandfather, and started his own car lot, Canyon Road Car Company. Joe and Jill went on to have two more daughters, Justine and Jaclyn, before divorcing in 2001.

Rod and high school had never clicked, and he dropped out before graduating. I might have contributed to his lack of interest in school, since he started having problems after I bought him a 1971 Mach 1 Mustang. I had felt guilty, leaving Rod to take care of his dad all the time, so I bought him a car, which he helped to pay for by hanging drapes for me. A couple of years later, he got his GED, and the teacher who gave him the test called to tell me he only missed one question, and how sorry she was that he hadn't finished high school.

That was the thing about Rod: He was truly gifted, but not in ways that showed up on a report card. He reminded me of Ralph in a lot of ways, even though Ralph hadn't been available to teach him all the things he knew how to do. Like Ralph, Rod could just figure things out. From a very young age, he could build or repair anything. He built furniture and gave the pieces as gifts. He could disassemble and reassemble an automobile, without a manual. When he found something he cared about, he was relentless, focused, and intense.

Dave Stipek connected Rod with people at Darigold, the Pacific Northwest's dairy marketing cooperative, and he got a job in Seattle. Rod was a young bachelor, out and about with his buddies all the time, and he liked to invite his crew over to our house for pool parties, especially when I wasn't around.

Meanwhile, my drapery business was bouncing back from the fire, and I was already thinking ahead. Both boys were grown: Joe was on his own, and Rod soon would be too. I spent my days in the pool house with my three assistants, cranking out orders, while Mary took care of Ralph. In the evenings it was just me, Ralph, and Rod (when he was home). On the nights when I had a meeting to attend, or somewhere I had to be, I would have a swing-shift nurse come, but I had to be home by 10:00 PM sharp, or they would leave. I called myself Cinderella then. Rod would also sit with Ralph many nights. The house that had always felt small and bustling felt bigger, quieter—almost too quiet.

In the spring of 1982, Ralph got pneumonia after accidentally aspirating some chicken noodle soup into his lungs. The infection turned serious, and he went downhill rapidly. He died on April 28, 1982.

The next weeks were a blur. The funeral. The reception in

the back yard. Mary, who'd been part of our family for eleven years, left to find another job.

My emotions were all over the place. Losing Ralph, and reminiscing with people at the funeral and reception, reminded me of everything I'd loved about him and our life together. He was such a rock: so strong, so capable, so humble, the perfect example for our boys. For nearly twenty years, I'd had the time of my life with him, adventuring out onto the Sound, hanging out with friends, raising the boys. But by the time I finally lost him, I'd been watching him die for more than a decade. It felt like he'd become a shadow of himself almost overnight, and then for eleven years every day was an ordeal: the pain, the limited movement, the frustrating lack of understanding and awareness of the world around him. After the shock of his death had faded somewhat, something strange hit me: I felt relieved for him, for finally reaching the end of his suffering. And I felt relieved for myself and the boys, that we no longer had to witness his struggle.

This sense of relief also brought some feelings of guilt with it. But mostly what I felt, in the weeks after Ralph's death, was loneliness. The house was all mine now, and it felt so different from when Ralph and I had built it nearly thirty years earlier. It felt big, empty, hollowed out. In the evenings, after my Cathy's Custom Décor crew had clocked out for the day, and I returned from our workspace to the empty house, the silence felt like a weight.

Dave Stipek and I were still good friends, but I didn't see him as much anymore. He was busy being the business agent for the Teamsters at all the dairies in the South Sound. We talked occasionally, especially after Ralph passed, and I visited him and his family a few times.

This wasn't the life I wanted: Waking up, heading to the backyard workshop, then returning to the empty house at night.

Public life had given me a chance to make a difference in other people's lives—but it had also made a huge difference in mine: I'd traveled around the country, met different people, learned about their lives, shared stories. I'd had a part in important decisions that affected people throughout the state. It had been exciting and rewarding. I'd returned to the drapery business out of desperation, because my family needed money to survive. But money wasn't enough.

So I started to look for a job that would open my life up a bit, get me out and about. I chatted with one of the employees at the wholesale place in Seattle where I'd been buying fabric and supplies.

"You know," she said, "we're always looking for salespeople. Why don't you apply?"

I thought it sounded like fun: Traveling to different businesses on the West Coast, meeting people and making sales. Plus, since I'd be on the road most of the time, I figured I could rent the house for some extra cash and stay at the pool house whenever I swung back through Tacoma. I threw my hat in the ring.

The company offered to fly me in to interview at their headquarters in San Francisco, and on the morning my flight was to leave, I called Dave to tell him the news.

"Why don't I pick you up from the airport later?" he said. "We'll have dinner."

I was shocked. In Olympia, Dave and I would only meet for dinner if he was taking another legislator out, and I was invited to join in his lobbying session. We saw each other at events all the time, but always drove separately. In Tacoma, we'd spend time with each other's families, but never went out alone together.

The interview went well, and I was offered the job on the spot. I was excited to share the news with Dave—but when I did, his face fell.

"I don't think it's a good idea," he said. "Why not stick with business here? You're doing great. It would be a shame to give it up now. It seems like a risky move, stepping away from a proven success to work for someone else."

I tried to sleep that night, but I kept thinking about the evening I'd just had with Dave. It had been a strange one: His dinner invitation; his discouragement of my taking a good-paying job. It didn't make sense. But given what I know now, I would have recognized what was going on: Dave had feelings for me that went beyond friendship. It may even have been that he didn't fully understand this himself, not yet. He'd invented some practical reasons why I shouldn't be away from him for weeks at a time, but the main reason he didn't want me to take the job was that I had become too important to him. I think I sensed this, even though I wasn't yet conscious of it, or fully aware of my own feelings for him. Dave remained completely devoted to Doris, and she was completely dependent on him, and I think both of us had blinders on in that regard. But it soon became apparent that Dave was starting to see a potential for more. In any case, I convinced myself that his objections made perfect sense. By morning, I'd decided to call and opt out of the job.

Thankfully, the house didn't stay silent for long after that. One night, when I came home from having dinner in Seattle with Dave and Doris, I found three couples—Rod, his date, and four others—in the pool. They were buck naked, loud as heck, and probably drunk. I was tired, and I didn't want to deal with it.

"Clothes on, everyone!" I said. "Party's over. I want everyone out of here."

They climbed out of the pool. Rod was mad. I'd embarrassed him in front of his friends, and of course, he had to lash out.

"Ah, shut up, Mom!" he said.

As soon as the words were out of his mouth, the woman

next to him punched him right in the face and he went down on the pool deck with a splat.

"Don't you talk to your mother like that!" the woman said. While she and the others put their clothes on, Rod lay on the pool deck. Blood poured from his nose.

I know love works in mysterious ways, but I didn't expect that Rod would fall head over heels for the woman who'd bloodied his nose. Her name was Shari and it turned out she had a thing for him, too. They started spending a lot of time together. She had an adorable two-year-old named Bradley, and whenever I was around, I would babysit him. Bradley and I became super-close, best friends.

Rod and Shari wanted to move in together, but finding a place big enough for the three of them wasn't in their budget.

I said, "I'm here all by myself. Why don't you just move in here?"

And they did. Bradley and I were inseparable whenever I was home, and Rod doted on him, too. Later on, he even adopted him as his own son, making him officially my grandson. Rod and Shari stayed with me for a while, before eventually moving out on their own. They had a daughter together, Jennifer, my second granddaughter.

Bradley and I are still best friends. We talk all the time.

For Thanksgiving that year, I hosted all the family I could fit into my house: Joe and Jill, Rod, Shari, Brad, and my mother. I loved having everyone under one roof, in a full and noisy house.

Later that evening, I got a call from Dave. It wasn't unusual for him to call on a holiday, so I didn't think anything of it.

"Happy Thanksgiving," I said.

"Happy Thanksgiving to you, too. I'm leaving Doris."

"What?"

If you didn't know Dave and Doris, it would be hard to understand: When they were married, he was a milk deliveryman, and Doris was very happy with that, with him coming home every day at a certain time and taking care of things around the house. But Dave was a bold person, and had built himself quite a career, from milkman to a business agent and big-shot lobbyist with connections all over the State of Washington. Doris would have preferred that he remained a milkman. She didn't like him being away, and she didn't like attending public events with him.

But Dave had grown and changed. When our families got together, I could see the relationship was one-sided. It wasn't that Doris was a selfish person. She was a sweet, lovely woman. And because of her health issues, she was almost childlike. But I think Dave liked to have someone to argue with once in a while, someone who wouldn't hesitate to challenge him. It was more complicated than that, of course. It always is.

Despite that Thanksgiving Day bombshell, I thought there was no way Dave would ever follow through. I invited Dave, Doris, and Cori to a Christmas Eve dinner at my home, and they seemed fine—which I thought was a little weird, given that he'd recently told her he was leaving. *No way*, I thought, *is he really going to do it.*

But he did. Cori was still at home to look after Doris, so she was in good hands.

In the coming months, Dave and I got closer and started to acknowledge our feelings for each other. He had planned to get an apartment on his own, but realized he couldn't afford it. So on February 3, 1983, he moved in with me. We were now a couple. Joe and Rod took a truck to Seattle and brought Dave and his belongings to our home in Tacoma.

* ✺ *

With the boys grown and gone and Dave by my side, I began

to think of myself as a grandmother not only to my own sons' kids—Joe's new daughter, Jamie, and Rod's stepson Bradley—but also to Dave's grandkids. I began a few family traditions—one of them completely by accident. Every year, a few days before Christmas, The Peoples Store, a department store in downtown Tacoma, hosted a Breakfast with Santa, where you could reserve a table for four and the kids could visit with Santa after your meal. It beat standing in line at the store, I thought. So the first Christmas after Dave moved in, I told Bradley and Dave's grandsons—at the time there were just two Stipek grandkids, Richard and David—that we were going to have Breakfast with Santa. They were so excited!

But I'd made a mistake: I hadn't checked with Peoples first. They were sold out. So I knew Breakfast with Santa would have to be at my home. I could handle the breakfast—Dave would make his signature corn pancakes, with eggs, bacon, and sausage—but I needed a Santa. Fortunately, at one of my political meetings, I met a man who played Santa at one of the local department stores, and he said he would come.

That first Christmas with Santa turned into an event that I hosted every Christmas for ten years, and soon included not only our grandkids, but the kids of many people I'd worked with in local and state government. All the judges' kids came, and by the tenth year, there wasn't any floor space available for all the children in the living room. Our Santa, in costume, would stop at a car parked up the street, where we'd stashed a bag of gifts the parents had bought, and he would throw the bag over his shoulder and come walking down the street, shouting: "Ho, ho ho! Merry Christmas!" When the kids heard his voice, they all ran to the window to see him heading to our door.

It meant a lot to me, the fact that I'd been able to hang on to that house through Ralph's sickness and eventual death, and I liked to celebrate it by hosting big get-togethers like this. In the years to come, it became a tradition for the family to gather at our place for big dinners, celebrating birthdays or holidays like the Fourth of July. There were usually more than a dozen family members present at a time, and I would cook up a batch of my specialty, spaghetti—or, if it was summer, Dave would grill steaks topped with sauteed mushrooms while the kids romped in the pool. I would go all out, making each dinner as special as I could, with a table set with my best china and crystal—and by the time my grandkids were teenagers, they all knew how to properly set a formal table. Eventually I had five Pearsall grandkids: Bradley and Jennifer from Rod and Shari and three granddaughters from Joe and Jill: Jamie, Justine, and Jaclyn. Dave had seven on his side, my step-grandkids: Richard, David, Rachel, Danny, Amy, Campbell, and Colleen.

I was loving life with Dave and my growing family. The house no longer felt empty, and I began to think about more than just getting by. Trying something new didn't seem scary, and I decided to reach for a way to contribute again, to do something. . . bigger, maybe, and more important. A return to public service felt like an obvious choice.

Later that year, I learned that Dave Tuell—the man who'd defeated me in my 1970 school board campaign—had decided not to run for reelection, leaving an open seat. This was a great chance, I thought, to both make up for that loss and put my experience and passion for education to good use.

I told Dave I wanted to run for the open seat on the Tacoma School Board. He had a concern, though. Before Ralph died, I'd been diagnosed with an abdominal hernia. And in the months that followed, it had worsened and become serious. If I fell, the doctor told me, it could rupture, and I could die.

Dave said: "I think you'd be great for the board. But if you don't get that hernia fixed, I don't think you should run."

I scheduled the operation as early as I could, but it was still cutting things close to the filing deadline. I spent a few days recovering—and then, on the last possible day, I went down to the County-City Building, filled out the paperwork, and put my name in.

I didn't have the energy to do much else: no campaign launch; no mailers or events; no volunteers from door to door. The frontrunner was a local businessman named John Lynn. A school board committee regular, he was knowledgeable, with lots of connections. Everyone assumed he would simply walk away with the seat.

I was still very popular with the families of the district, though, and without any word from me, they rallied behind me. I shocked everyone by winning the primary. It meant I would be running unopposed in November.

Most of the other board members—who remembered me all too well from my PTA days, when I had been a real thorn in their sides—weren't exactly thrilled. They knew I didn't want to simply sit in meetings and listen to people talk about doing things; I wanted to actually do things, to make a difference for students and their families. One of the board members, Betty Drost, said she was going to quit if I was elected. Of course I was elected, and of course she didn't follow through on her threat. She and I later became good friends. At that time, oversight of the city's preschool and K–12 schools was just one of the Tacoma School District's responsibilities. It also oversaw the local vocational/technical schools. Soon after I was seated on the board, the superintendent came to me and asked if I would be interested in serving as a liaison between the board and Bates Technical College.

Bates had always held a special place in my heart: It had

given me and Ralph a leg up when we were a young couple, giving Ralph advice and guidance on the building of our house, and offering a certification program that helped me become a more effective leader. I thought of it as a champion for the "middle" students, the ones who didn't get all the fancy programs or attention or guidance that went to either special learning or college-bound kids. Public schools often forgot about them— kind of like I felt Rod had been lost in the high school shuffle. Bates had a lot to offer these students, and I jumped at the chance to get involved.

I was a busy liaison. I sat in on every meeting of its Board of Trustees. Bill Mohler, the president, convinced the board to seek funds from the state to build another campus to house more programs, like its Fire Services Training Center, steel or metal working programs, and others. The board wanted a big chunk of land to bring everything together on a single campus. Downtown Tacoma, unfortunately, didn't have the kind of site the college would need. The first piece of property Bates had picked turned out to be unsuitable, and the expansion was stuck in limbo.

Now, at the end of the hill where I lived in South Tacoma, there was a giant gravel pit that hadn't been used for years. When Joe and Rod were young boys, they liked to tear up and down its slopes on their dirt bikes. It was a massive piece of land, more than thirty acres, with easy access to the free-way. It seemed like a perfect spot for a school, with plenty of room to grow.

I told the other board members about it, and eventually con-vinced them that this was where the new Bates South Campus needed to be. The city bought the land, and we held a meeting at Arlington Elementary with the neighbors to discuss their concerns. They had only one major concern, which was traffic. The district, the city, and the neighborhood all worked together to approve a design that addressed their concerns.

In the spring of 1985, construction of the Bates South Campus began. Because it was practically in my back yard, I became a regular visitor (I was even given my own hard hat), touring the property and checking in with neighbors to see how they were feeling about everything.

Everything was on track for a grand opening in 1987, until a wrench got thrown into the works: Tacoma's United Steel-workers Union, Local 237, went on strike. This held up some of the project's finishing touches, like the garage doors. They couldn't be built and installed without steelworkers.

I didn't want to delay the opening of our South Campus, so I called the leader of the Local 237, and their head of labor relations, and asked them to meet with me.

I explained the situation to them, how important it was to get the campus opened in time for the coming semester. "Look," I said. "Since your guys can't work on this right now, maybe we use some of our students, the ones training in steelwork? They could install the doors under your supervision and guidance." This way, nobody would be crossing picket lines, and the work would still be done by future union members.

It turned out the union guys weren't any happier than I was about delaying the opening of a school that trained future steelworkers. They were on board with finding a solution, and this seemed to suit everyone. The deal was struck, the students installed the doors, and the Bates South Campus opened on schedule.

The South Campus has been a massive success story for Tacoma and its vo-tech students. It's by far the biggest and busiest of the college's three campuses, with nearly 250,000 square feet of building space serving thousands of students and community members.

⁂

My work on the Bates South Campus almost didn't get done, though, because of something that happened in the spring of 1984: I received a property tax assessment that told me the value of my home had jumped 17 percent in one year.

It had been three years since Pierce County had combined the offices of assessor—the official who valued properties for taxation purposes—and treasurer, who levied those taxes. Nobody seemed particularly happy with the change. I know I wasn't. How did the assessor arrive at these valuations? Nobody had ever visited my property, to my knowledge. Why was it that homeowners were seeing their taxes increase 17 percent in one year, while business owners seemed to be paying about the same year to year?

I was so outraged by the notice that in July, I announced my candidacy against the incumbent assessor-treasurer, Sheldon Cook, a Republican. I had a campaign mailer printed up that featured, on one side, an exact copy of the notice I'd been sent, showing the increase. Above the new assessment, in bold text, was printed the question: "Has Your Property Tax Gone Skyhigh Without Any Explanation?" Cook's office, apparently, had received hundreds of complaints from Pierce County homeowners, demanding answers about their own increases. They weren't satisfied with the answer: The assessor-treasurer's computer had made the increases, based on increases in the value of similar properties. What were those increases based on? What similar properties? Nobody seemed to know.

I printed up tens of thousands of these mailers. Because the State Democratic Party was paying postage, they had to be mailed out of Seattle. So we got Joe's van and we loaded it up with big gray canvas bags (Property of U.S. Postal Service) full of the fliers, and sent him off to Seattle—but the van broke down on the way. A few campaign workers and I drove up to help offload the bags into our cars, and finished the trip from there.

The mailers got a lot of attention. Some voters were confused—they thought they were getting a new property tax assessment, and they called the assessor-treasurer's office with questions. The flyer was clearly marked as campaign literature, and on the other side was printed a direct message from me to the voters. The *Tacoma News Tribune* wrote a story about the flyers, in which Sheldon Cook called me "that brazen woman." I was happy to be able to lay out the case for my campaign in a news article. Homeowners were shouldering a disproportionate amount of the county's tax burden—while some of their properties hadn't been inspected for more than a decade! Things needed to change.

I had already thought about my position on the school board, and what might happen if I were elected assessor-treasurer. I asked Senator Bottiger's office to advise me on whether it was a conflict of interest, and within a few days, received a letter from a member of the Senate Judiciary Committee saying he didn't think it would be a problem. So I announced my candidacy and began campaigning—but a few weeks after that I received another letter, from one of the assistant state attorneys general. A 1917 court case, he said, had found that the two positions were incompatible—and also, he wrote, the treasurer was responsible for receiving and holding all the money belonging to the school districts. Reluctantly, I decided I would have to resign my position on the school board if I won the election.

It was an incredibly close contest. On election night, I held a slim lead, but Cook had taken his own slim lead by the next morning. After more than 36,000 absentee ballots were counted, I had lost the election by a few hundred votes.

A few weeks later, while I was working on some drapes with my employees, Joe showed up. He was carrying a big gray canvas postal bag, stuffed full of mail.

"Mom," he said. "Look what I found crammed behind the seat in the van."

The bag had gotten lost in the chaos while we were loading bags into our cars from the broken-down van. In it were all the mailers that were supposed to have gone to Gig Harbor, a heavily Democratic precinct, home to thousands of registered voters. There's no way to be sure, but I believe to this day that if those mailers had gone out to the voters of Gig Harbor, I would have been the next Pierce County assessor-treasurer.

It was tough, losing by such a slim margin after an avoidable mistake, and I wished better for Pierce County's homeowners. But I wasn't too upset. I still had a lot of work to do for Tacoma's schools.

Since 1965, Tacoma Public Schools had been involved in a program that made everyone in the city proud. When the U.S. State Department opened an independent school in Lagos, Nigeria—the American International School of Lagos (AISL)—Tacoma Schools partnered with the school to send teachers, funding, and expertise to Lagos. It's the longest school-to-school partnership the State Department has ever had, and it's still going strong today.

The school teaches students from preschool to high school, and is located on Victoria Island, in the heart of Lagos's swanky financial district. It offers once-in-a-lifetime opportunities to teachers from Tacoma, who move their families to Nigeria, totally immerse themselves in a completely different world, and learn about different people and cultures. And for a select group of Nigerian students, attending AISL means getting a top-notch American-style education. They graduate with both an American high school diploma and the International Baccalaureate, the global equivalent of an Advanced Placement program. These degrees open doors to some of the world's most competitive colleges and universities. For a kid to make it onto the roster of AISL is a huge accomplishment in itself.

Every year, the AISL invited a Tacoma School Board member to Lagos to meet with the board and talk about ways the two schools could work together to benefit the students. The AISL school board was different from ours—it was composed mostly of international business executives with connections to the State Department, people from companies like Arco and Standard Oil. They didn't have a ton of educational experience, but they knew how to get things done.

In 1987, it was my turn to travel to Nigeria and work with their board. They would fly me first-class to Lagos, and I would stay for two weeks, working with the superintendent. It sounded like a real adventure—but I wasn't sure I wanted to go. One evening, at home, Dave and I were lounging in the pool with a couple of our neighbors, Pat and Gordie, and I told them about it.

"You have to go," Pat said.

"The hell we do," Dave said. "I traveled all over the world when I was in the Navy, and it gets old fast."

Pat wouldn't let it go. She loved traveling, visiting and learning about different corners of the world. "You should do everything you can to go," she said. "You'll never regret it. If you have to mortgage your house, you should go."

We thought about it. A first-class ticket to Lagos was already paid for. I thought it might be fun, and Dave didn't need too much convincing. We decided to tack a vacation onto the tail end of the trip, to go on safari in Kenya and see a little bit of Europe on our way back home.

One of the things we were told was that the American teachers really missed good chocolate candy—and that M&Ms were the only kind that could make it through the heat. They were melt-proof.

We arrived in Lagos on a day in October, and it hit us right away: This place was much, much different from South Tacoma. We were greeted at the airport by the superintendent of the district (there's a second State Department school in the Nigerian capital, Abuja), Stan Jacobsen, and his wife Ebba—and by dozens of uniformed soldiers. Each of the men carried a rifle with a bayonet, and when one of them checked our passports, I couldn't help feeling a little uneasy. The country had recently been placed under martial law. Since the mid-1960s, Nigeria's government had suffered five successful coups, and a few other unsuccessful attempts. And just months before our arrival, the regime—which had come to power by staging its own coup in 1985—had thwarted an overthrow and executed more than a dozen of the plotters. So things were tense, and the soldiers with bayonets were meant to be intimidating. There were curfews in effect, limiting the times people could be out walking the streets. It was like something out of a movie.

The school was like a dream, an oasis inside an oasis, a beautiful campus with immaculate classrooms and outdoor spaces, all tucked into Lagos's fanciest neighborhood. The Tacoma teachers were lined up at the door when I arrived, waiting for their M&Ms. The students were bright and charming. They greeted me and Dave with a dance routine, and several of them tried to drag me out onto the floor with them. I laughed it off. I'm not much of a performer, at least when it comes to dance.

Most of my "on" time at the school was spent with Stan and the other board members, and sometimes the teachers, talking over issues and hammering out solutions. But I also visited the classrooms whenever I could, to get an understanding of what the students were learning, and what they needed in order to learn better. I loved hanging out with the kids. One little girl liked to pull me aside whenever I visited her class, to read to me from her latest book. I could tell she was so proud.

Stan and Ebba were two of the kindest, most generous people we could have hoped to meet. They drove us all over Lagos, showing us the sights. The school was just a few blocks from the beach, and we spent several evenings out there with them, other board members, and teachers, just hanging out. It reminded me a bit of my carefree days with the Tacoma Outboard Association—except way hotter. Even the ocean was warm.

In the mornings, while Stan and I were at work, Ebba was kind enough to invite Dave for walks through the neighborhoods of Victoria Island. Here, even in the city's most upscale area—Its center of business and high finance—sewage ran openly through gutters and roadside canals. Every day, Dave would see children literally fishing, with poles and baited hooks, for their next meal in these sewers. Ebba would chat with people they met along the way. Dave said it seemed like Stan and Ebba knew everyone and everything in Lagos.

One of the things that surprised me most about Lagos was how the rich and poor live right on top of each other—unlike America, where they hardly see each other. One night Dave and I joined one of the board members, along with Ebba and Stan, at a local nightclub. To get in, we stepped over an open sewer, entered a rundown-looking building, and got on an elevator. And when the doors opened at the top floor, my jaw nearly hit the floor: The club was plush and exquisite, like something you'd see in a Manhattan penthouse. Afterward, we went with one of the board members to his house: a mansion, with gates patrolled by security guards and dogs, right next to the open sewer where people fished for their dinners. It made such an impression on me that I wrote home to Joe and Rod and tried to explain it: "Here," I wrote, "you can open a gate and step from a garbage dump into a palace."

Our two weeks in Lagos flew by. When we were on the plane to Kenya, and out of Nigerian airspace, the flight attendants served champagne. When we got to Kenya, we were met by the woman who oversaw all the African schools in the State Department program, and she took us to her home to change for the flight to the safari, which was an amazing experience. On our return, we were met by the same gal, and she put us on a train called the "Lunatic Express" to Mombasa. It stopped at every little village on its way, where people on the train threw money to the people on the tracks.

Dave and I enjoyed the rest of our trip—but everywhere we went after Lagos, I felt more like a tourist. Mombasa is a beautiful port city, a centuries-old trading center—but its economy revolves around tourism now. I loved every minute of our time in these places, but in Lagos, Stan and Ebba and the teachers and board members were members of a tight-knit community, and they made me and Dave feel like we were part of the family. It was a warm, wonderful feeling, and it changed my life forever. I think this is what Pat was trying to explain to me when she urged me to go to Africa—but it wasn't a feeling anyone could really explain to someone else. It was something I had to experience for myself. For many years, I thought about Lagos and its people every day. They forever changed the way I understood the world, the vast differences between its haves and have-nots, and how maybe, just maybe, we could come together to bridge that gap.

In Tacoma, even though I'd sent my kids to a magnet school in a neighborhood of mostly Black families, I'd never felt like an outsider—probably because I was focused on my family, our boys, and their well-being. But being a white person in a city of 4 million Black people (this was in 1987; Lagos is a now a megacity of more than 16 million) changed the way I saw things. It's hard to put into words: Everyone I met was kind, friendly, generous. But I couldn't shake the feeling of being different, an outsider looking in. It made me think more about how minorities experience life in America, and for sure, it impacted the political work I did in the years to come.

It's been nearly forty years since I visited the teachers and students of Lagos, and while I don't think about them every single day anymore, I still think about them a lot. They just pop into my head from time to time, when I see something in the world that reminds me of them.

❧

It was around this time that Dave and I started to talk about getting married. We were happy together, and satisfied with the status quo—but we were also very practical, both of us. There were a lot of sensible reasons to get married: For one, I was beginning to think I wanted to get back into politics, and the hard truth was that more voters would go for a married woman than they would for an unmarried woman who lived with her boyfriend.

There was no proposal or anything like that. We just talked it over and decided it was the thing to do. Maybe it wasn't very romantic, but the wedding day was an absolute joy. On June 13, 1989, Dave and I were married in a backyard ceremony, in the presence of our families and friends. It was a beautiful spring day in Tacoma, full of love and laughter. I was now Mrs. Cathy Pearsall-Stipek.

❧

The man whose smear campaign had taken my seat in the state legislature in 1978, Wendell Brown, hadn't lasted long in Olympia. People didn't like his style. He'd come back to Tacoma and gotten involved in Pierce County politics, serving on the county council until 1988, when he ran a successful campaign for Pierce County Assessor-Treasurer. When he took that position, he resigned his council seat, which meant the council needed to appoint someone to serve until the next election.

I'd served on the Tacoma School Board for six years, and had several achievements to show for it—and now I saw a chance to get involved in real governance again, to serve a constituency and solve problems.

This was how interim appointments to the council worked: The county precinct committee, comprised of representatives from each Pierce County precinct, met to pick three names they would forward to the County Council for consideration. I had a good reputation for getting things done in Pierce County, so I earned most of the nominations. I think it was eighty-nine or ninety people who nominated me. Five nominated another guy whose name I can't remember. Two nominated a person named Miriam Graves. Miriam had worked in food service for Tacoma Schools, and was a member of the League of Women Voters. She seemed like a nice woman. But she'd never been active in the Democratic Party.

The precinct committee's vote wasn't a mandate; it was a suggestion. The council members could appoint anyone they wanted. I knew a few of the people in the Democratic majority, and I visited one of them, Dennis Flannigan, soon before the council was scheduled to meet. I told him how excited I was by the idea of serving on the council, and I shared my ideas for things the council could do to address problems in the community.

I made a mistake at Dennis's house that I would never make again: I assumed he and I were friends, and I didn't ask him to say, explicitly, that he would support me as the appointee.

It turned out that Dennis was like a lot of Big Boys: He liked to sit in a big chair and talk about big things, but he didn't really like to do any of those things. He didn't like making decisions that might ruffle feathers. He liked his title, and his position.

On the day they were picking the new council member, I went to the County-City Building with the other candidates to watch the show—but there wasn't much of a show.

As soon as the meeting was gaveled in, Chuck Gorden—he was the only Republican on the council—made the motion that they were appointing Miriam Graves. And that was that. The council voted unanimously for Miriam Graves.

I won't waste time guessing why they did it, but it seemed pretty obvious to me. After the meeting, Miriam and I shared an awkward elevator ride down to the lobby. I made it more awkward when I said: "Enjoy your new job, Miriam. Because I'm going to take it away from you in November."

It turns out I didn't have to put up much of a fight, and I would have felt sorry for Miriam. . . if she'd run against anyone else. I don't think she'd ever run a campaign in her life. I had supporters all over the county. The dozens of people who supported me in the precinct committee were all on board, and all my other friendships and connections made for an easy win over Miriam in the August primary. I won the general election in November of 1989—and, because Miriam Graves's appointment expired that month, I would be sworn in right away. I was thrilled. But the other council members? Not so much.

I now knew they, including Dennis Flannigan, didn't want me anywhere near them. But I wasn't expecting things to get so frosty right off the bat. After the election, I called the Chief Clerk of the Council, Gerri Rainwater—whom I knew, and had always gotten along with—and asked if I could swing by to see my new office. She told me the other council members wouldn't let me do that while Miriam was still using it. Apparently, I would have to wait until I was sworn in on November 22. My first look at the office would be my first day on the job. "Well, okay then. I guess I'll just have to wait," I said.

Dave and I planned my swearing-in ceremony to be at our home. But guess what? That morning, as we were getting ready to welcome our guests, I found out the council had called a special meeting to be held that same day—knowing I wouldn't be able to attend, as I would be busy with the ceremony. It was irritating, to say the least. As soon as I got sworn in and took my oath, I bolted for the County-City Building, leaving everyone else to enjoy the after-party, and joined the other council members for their "special meeting."

"I'm here!" I said. The other council members seemed surprised to see me.

Gerri Rainwater showed me to my office. There was a desk, a chair—and nothing else, not even a paper clip. The office had been completely stripped before I'd shown up.

My eyes went to the window, where I saw the ugliest drapes I'd ever seen. And I recognized them immediately! They were the drapes from the auditorium at the Tacoma Schools building, drapes I'd hated so passionately that I'd complained about them constantly, for years. I'd even asked one of the other school board members to change seats with me during our meetings, so I wouldn't have to look at them.

"Gerri," I said. "What the hell is this?"

Gerri didn't seem to get it. The drapes weren't just ugly; they were poorly made. They were supposed to be pleated drapes, but these drapes didn't hold the pleats, and they ballooned out. They didn't hang right at all. Nobody at the school board had bothered to tell the draper to come back and do it right, and nobody had done anything about them. For years!

And now here they were. I thought: Did the council members really hate me this much? Enough to go dig up these awful drapes and throw them in my face?

Look, I wouldn't have minded having a stapler or two around—you know, the basics. But I'd been left to my own devices before. Stripping the office was a childish gesture, but now I had a clear picture of what I was getting myself into.

The drapes, on the other hand, turned out to be a friend messing with me. The custodian for the council's quarters was a man named Dick, who happened to be the brother of my childhood friend Wanda, who'd lived near my grandparents' house. Dick was good friends with the custodian at the Tacoma Schools building. My hatred of those drapes had apparently become legendary, and the other custodian told Dick about it. They thought it would be funny to hang them in my new office.

Dick would become one of my few allies in the years to come, one of a handful who gave a damn about doing his job. Whatever I needed done, he would do it. If I told him I needed a room painted, he would ask me what color, and get to work.

The first thing I asked him to do was take down those godawful drapes.

CHAPTER 10

An Ineffective Council Births Political Tigress

(1989–1993)

MY FELLOW PIERCE COUNTY Council members' reception of me was a taste of things to come. The seven of us would never really get along, and trying to get anything done felt like pulling teeth. I showed up at my office every day and put my nose to the grindstone, gathering information, reaching out to constituents, trying to learn the best way forward on all the issues we faced. Most of the men only came into the office on meeting days. That is, until Sally Walker, a former state representative, joined the council in the summer of 1990. Sally was the only Republican on the council, but she was really a breath of fresh air. She took her job seriously, and the two of us hit it off.

There were heaps of problems that needed solving in Pierce County. Land use decisions, for one, were a tangled mess: I thought development projects got the green light without much study, and I thought the county needed to do a better job of weighing the pros and cons. It was impossible for the other council members to make an informed decision. They seemed more worried about how the votes would play out in the next election than in actually finding solutions.

I ended up chairing the Public Works Committee, and one issue became the perfect symbol of how the council dodged tough choices: Our landfill was overflowing, and we needed to expand capacity.

LeMay's Refuse was the garbage contractor for Pierce County. I liked the owner, Harold LeMay. He was good at his job, and I had always found him to be one of the most honest and sincere people to deal with. Harold could be a bit of a bulldog when he was going after what he wanted, though, and the other council members didn't seem to like his style. Instead of doing the simple, sensible thing, the council asked for proposals from companies that would haul our garbage off and bury it in Oregon or Eastern Washington. I was the only one who came out against the idea. I thought it put us at the mercy of outside interests. I thought we ought to be handling our own damned garbage. But this was the way the council worked: They kicked their problems down the road and let someone else deal with it. Bury the trash, bury the problem.

Harold would later receive an award from the National Waste and Recycling Association for his management of our landfill—and since nobody on the council wanted to see him receive that award, I was proud to be the one who represented the council and joined Harold for the award ceremony in Washington, D.C.

The council members barely saw each other outside of meetings, so no real discussions ever took place. It was all posturing. When it came time to review the County Charter—the rulebook for how the county executive and council governed together—nobody wanted to sit on the three-person committee. It was a political minefield, tasked with recommendations on some hot-button issues, including whether to lengthen the two-term limit for elected offices.

I volunteered to head this committee; most of the others ran for the hills. Eventually I was joined by two others, Paul Cyr and Barbara Gelman. We made good progress and were on track to bring some proposed changes to the charter for the November 1991 election. But then I left town for a few days, and while I was gone, Paul and Barbara decided to bring the five changes straight to the full council, for a vote to decide on whether they should even go to the voters. Can you believe that?! A vote on whether the voters should vote!

On top of that, Paul and Barbara dropped a proposed change we'd all agreed on: creating an independent commission to set county officials' salaries. It made more sense than politicians deciding their own paychecks. This move really ticked me off, and as a result our debates on that issue ate up even more time. In the end, the council voted not to put any of the proposed changes before the voters. As the chair of the charter review committee, I was embarrassed, and I apologized publicly to the people of Pierce County.

I tried to answer every letter from my constituents, but it was a one-woman show. The council wouldn't allow me to hire my own aide. Use the existing staff, they said.

Fine, I thought. Soon the council staff was drowning in constituent mail, barely able to keep up with anyone else's work. The brilliant solution was to form a three-person committee to answer the mail together: me, Dennis Flannigan, and Chuck Gorden. Dennis and Chuck were not my biggest fans, so I was prepared for the worst, but once they saw how much more mail I was answering, they decided I could have my own assistant—but nobody else could.

So I reached out to Joan Rutherford and convinced her to

come work with me again. And her arrival at the City-County Building soon triggered an all-out war.

For about a year, the council and the county executive, Joe Stortini—the former high school football coach—had been talking about remodeling our tenth-floor office spaces. It would have been a running joke, but it wasn't funny. We and the staff were crammed in like sardines, and we really needed to reconfigure the spaces. When Joan joined me, there was literally nowhere for her to work. The council staff gave her a desk and chair and set her up in the hallway, just outside my office door. She was right next to the restroom.

It was such a stupid move—tone-deaf and a little mean-spirited, I thought. I asked for a meeting to decide how to create separate workspaces for our staff, but unsurprisingly, our "study session" resulted in no timeline—no concrete plans at all.

So I did what I always do when I think change is needed: I took what some might call extreme action. I told Joan to move into my office, where she could get some work done, and I moved myself out to her desk in the hall. Somebody had recently given me a near-life-size stuffed tiger, and I set it down next to me as a barrier to keep people from walking behind me. I was a strange sight to behold, and the *Tacoma News Tribune* got wind of it and sent a reporter and a photographer out. The story in the paper ("Tight Office Space Plops Councilwoman in Corridor") was accompanied by a picture of me at the desk, talking on the phone, while the tiger stood guard and two women tried to squeeze past me down the hallway.

The other council members were furious: I'd made a public issue of their refusal to act and make simple decisions. Joe Stortini was livid, especially when the reporter called him for comment. I told the reporter all I was trying to do was give Joan a place where she could work in peace and quiet. But I knew what I was doing. The article forced Joe and the council to confront two uncomfortable questions: Why didn't the staff have enough room to work? And why was I the only one with an assistant?

Within six months, every council member had their own assistant. There was no way the council or Joe Stortini wanted a photo in the paper showing seven assistants huddled in the hallway. The tenth-floor remodel became a priority and was soon completed.

One of the County Council's many obligations was appointing judges, and when a district court judgeship opened up in early 1992, I knew just the guy for the job: my friend John McCarthy. John was a lawyer who'd served ten years as one of the Port of Tacoma's commissioners. His wife Pat had served on the Tacoma School Board with me, and we'd become good friends. I knew John was as qualified as anyone, so I went to five of the other members—there were seven of us on the council—and secured their commitment to him. That left Dennis Flannigan. We weren't exactly on each other's Christmas card lists, and I didn't need his vote, so I skipped him.

So with John's judgeship locked in, we headed into the meeting. Imagine my surprise when I saw another friendly face in the room: Ron Culpepper, whom I'd known since the late 1970s, when he'd chaired our district's Democratic party. I thought: What is Ron doing here? But before I could ask, the meeting began.

Dennis opened the meeting and proposed Ron for the judgeship—and seemed genuinely shocked to learn most of us had lined up behind John, who won the appointment easily.

I was happy for John, but I felt awful for Ron. I called him after the vote, apologized, and explained what had happened. Apparently, Dennis Flannigan had simply chosen a candidate he thought everyone would rubber-stamp, even me, and never bothered mentioning it: So typical, I thought.

So in the spring of 1992, we came up with an idea we hoped would improve our performance: We, all seven of us, would spend a few days together, holed up at a hotel on the Hood Canal, with the goal of getting to the bottom of our dysfunctional chaos and setting things right. We even invited a *News Tribune* reporter to take notes and report on our retreat, to show the public we were serious about being accountable.

One troublesome issue we identified was our current chairman, Paul Cyr, who was arrogant and sneaky, withholding information from the rest of us. Anything that might sway someone to vote against his pet projects would stay buried in his desk drawer. Another issue was that people were always late, including one member who'd singlehandedly torpedoed several meetings. She had trouble getting out of bed in the morning, she said. And another concern was, as the *News Tribune* article put it: "Pearsall-Stipek, who has a reputation for speaking her mind even if it means publicly criticizing her colleagues."

Councilman Cyr complained that I could be "truck driver-ish."

The reporter recorded my response perfectly: "I admit I can be a bitch," I said. "But I'm a bitch when things aren't going the way they should be."

At the end of the retreat, we managed to accomplish one thing: We gave ourselves a grade of "unsatisfactory." And everyone went home to Tacoma without a plan to make our work more satisfactory.

I had never been part of a more ineffective group and I couldn't stand it. I wanted out.

I started to pull away from the County Council after that spring retreat, partly because I didn't see how anything was going to get better. I felt like I'd been beating my head against a wall for three years—and for what?

Cartoon by Chris Britt.
Reprinted with permission

By that time, the presidential campaign of 1992 was heating up, and I saw a chance to do something useful, to actually make a difference, for the Democratic candidate, Arkansas Governor Bill Clinton. The Washington State Democratic Party, headquartered in Seattle, appointed a fresh-faced Young Democrat to run our district's campaign. This was their usual procedure—I guess they liked to have things run by someone perky, energetic, and totally inexperienced. Someone more likely to fall in line and take direction from Seattle.

I called this new campaign manager and peppered him with questions I knew he wouldn't be able to answer: Where would he set up the office? What kind of materials would he produce? How were they going to connect with voters? He had no idea.

"You don't really know what you're doing, do you?" I said.

He replied: "I don't really want to do this, to be honest."

"Well, good," I said. "How about I do it instead?"

"That would be great. I'd love that."

Dave and I became co-chairs and took over the Clinton/Gore

campaign for the 6th Congressional District. I knew a realtor who hooked us up with an empty storefront on 84th Street. We set up our headquarters there and started printing T-shirts, buttons, and signs to sell to our supporters. Dave and I each loaned a thousand dollars of our own money to the campaign to get things rolling, and we were up and running. Not long after we'd taken charge of the district, Dave and I, along with the other district campaign managers, were invited to meet Governor Clinton in Seattle. We didn't get a lot of face time, but it was an honor I'll never forget. I still have photos of Dave and me at the event.

Cathy meeting Bill Clinton when
he was running for President

When Seattle found out we were making and selling our own merchandise, they were livid, of course—at least for a few days, until they realized they hadn't ordered their own stuff in time for the big Clinton/Gore open house. Someone from their office called and asked if we had any shirts, buttons. . . anything.

"Yeah," I said. "We do."

Dave and I and a couple other staffers took our stuff up to Seattle, to the open house, and it all sold out, every last item.

Each month, the Clinton/Gore campaign sent surrogates to each state to find out how things were going. The surrogates started showing up at our office with buttons they'd snagged from other campaign offices around the country, for us to copy and sell. I had my own button guy and he took theirs apart, made bootleg copies, and started cranking them out by the hundreds. We sold so many, the campaign was running a surplus.

With the election heating up, I decided to call all the Democratic precinct committee people in the county to offer my staff's help with their campaigns, especially in their door-to-door canvasses. I did this for two reasons: I wanted to do everything I could to notch a win for the Clinton/Gore campaign, of course, but I also wanted to put myself in front of these precinct leaders.

Pierce County's auditor, Brian Sonntag, was running for the position of Washington State Auditor, and he had a good chance of winning. He was a Democrat from a well-heeled political family; his father had been Pierce County Auditor for more than twenty years. Brian had also been among the Pierce County Young Democrats, the Big Boys–in-training, who didn't like my truck driver-ish style or my lack of pedigree.

County Auditor was a plum job, involving lots of ways to serve the public. In Washington's second-largest county, the auditor oversaw all elections, provided licensing services, and kept public records. I thought I could do a lot of good there—and I loved the idea of escaping the county council.

It seemed doable: Brian Sonntag wouldn't have a say in who replaced him. Like all county appointments, the next auditor would be picked from one of three candidates recommended to the county council by the precinct committee. The council would make the final call: I would be recused, of course, and I knew the other council members would vote enthusiastically to shove me out the door.

So, together with Dave and our staff, I hit the sidewalks

with the people working these precincts, showering them with campaign swag—shirts and buttons and signs. The precinct committee leaders ate it up. They were really grateful, and they let me know it.

We kept selling things right and left. Our surplus grew even more. So we rented an RV and hit the road, taking all the state candidates' signs and campaign materials with us to bring to voters all over the State of Washington. We put our candidates in front of thousands of voters.

When we wrapped up our statewide barnstorm, we still had money left, so in the lunchroom of the new Bates South Campus, we hosted a big dinner for all the campaign workers in the district. Everyone agreed it was one of the best-run campaigns in the state.

The November 1992 election was a good one for the Democrats: Bill Clinton won the presidency. Brian Sonntag was the new Washington State Auditor. Before the results had even been called, I told a *News Tribune* reporter I expected Brian to win, and that I was throwing my hat in the ring to be his successor.

I'm sure there was some pearl-clutching at the idea that somebody would make this announcement before the results were final, but I didn't have to be discreet. I'd already done the work I needed to lock down the appointment, and I'd left nothing to chance: On election night, I mailed out a letter to every Democratic precinct committee member, all the people I'd helped on the campaign trail, and asked them to support me if the auditor's office became vacant. They were practically tripping over themselves to get behind me. I visited each of my fellow county council members, and I'm telling you their faces lit up at the prospect of my leaving the council chamber for a new office elsewhere. They were absolutely tickled pink. I could count on them, they said.

Of course, after the dust settled, it dawned on a few others—including Joe Stortini, who'd been term-limited out of office, and councilman Dennis Flannigan—that they wanted the appointment. Brian Sonntag wanted anyone but me to be his successor, but his efforts to thwart me were, like everyone else's effort, too little, too late. He scrambled to find another candidate, and to buy time, so he asked the county's Democratic chairman Bill Baarsma to delay the precinct committee's nomination meeting. It didn't work. The committee's support of me was overwhelming; there was no way anyone was going to get away with appointing someone else. Dennis saw the writing on the wall, and along with every other member of the council, he voted to appoint me as the new Pierce County Auditor.

Before each of us officially took office in January, I called Brian and asked him to meet with me, so I could ask him a few questions and get some advice. I also wanted to smooth things over a bit, if I could, and show him I was serious about the job. I met him and his deputy auditor, Ken Radkey, for lunch, and asked him for any nuggets of wisdom for running the office.

Brian nodded at his deputy and said, "I mostly just let Ken handle the details."

I was blown away. The job had to be the busiest government job in the county: Elections, marriage, auto, and boat licenses. Records. It was all very public-facing and very, very demanding. I asked Ken: "So what do you do, then?"

"Oh," he said, "I usually grab the newspaper first thing in the morning and get coffee, and read up on current events for a bit. Then I sit down and look through the budget to see how we're doing. And we're usually doing fine. That's pretty much the job."

They might have been telling the truth: Maybe neither of them was very interested in doing the work. Or there was the other possibility that they wanted to avoid giving me anything they thought might help me succeed. Or—more likely—it might have been a little of both.

So in mid-January of 1993, after Brian Sonntag was sworn in, I prepared to be sworn in as Pierce County Auditor. I resigned my seat on the council—to this day I wonder whether the other council members threw a party afterwards—and announced my first two hires to the *News Tribune*: My trusty assistant, Joan Rutherford, and my deputy auditor, John Gamble. John had gone to school with Joe, and he had political connections all over the county, including friendships with the former county executive and the mayor of Tacoma. Given his connections, I wondered why nobody had snatched him up for a political job after the election. Without asking around, I offered John the position of deputy auditor, and he agreed.

As I would find out soon enough, I should have asked around.

CHAPTER 11

You Can't Do That! Challenging Pierce County's Political Establishment

(1993)

JOAN AND JOHN WERE my only two hires in my new role as Pierce County Auditor. The rest of the staff were permanent county staff, and I was thankful to have them aboard, as I was new to the position and appreciated their experience and insight.

It wasn't long after I'd stepped into my office for the first time, and was preparing to be sworn in by Judges Healy and McCarthy, that I looked up and saw Art, a political acquaintance, coming through the door. I'd seen him at a few different political events before, but I didn't really know him.

"Thanks for coming," I said. "You're just in time for the ceremony."

"I'm your new deputy auditor," he said. "Doug Sutherland sent me to be sworn in."

I smelled trouble. Doug Sutherland was the new Republican county executive, the former mayor of Tacoma. Apparently he thought he would be the one to hire my deputy. At first I just thought it was odd—maybe he didn't know I'd already hired

John? It didn't seem likely. I had mentioned my new hires to the press.

I told Art thanks for stopping by, but I already had a deputy. And I sent him on his way. I didn't hear from Doug Sutherland for a while. I assumed he was letting it go. I thought in my days on the County Council I'd seen about the worst the Big Boys could throw at me. But I hadn't seen anything yet.

As the first payday approached, one of my staff noticed that the names Joan Rutherford and John Gamble weren't on the payroll. I checked it out. And I saw that the two new hires made by Barbara Gelman, the newly elected assessor-treasurer, had also been excluded.

I was pretty steamed, and I called Doug right away.

It seemed Doug Sutherland had a theory about his power as the county executive: He saw himself as a sort of king who ruled over every county officer—even those who, like him, were elected by the people. In his mind, our authority to do what we were elected to do—to hire people, even to set the policies we'd campaigned on—was subject to his approval. Apparently, Joan and John's names weren't on the payroll because I hadn't bent the knee and gotten Doug's approval.

It was stupid. No county executive had ever tried to grab that much power. And I told him so.

"What you've done is disgusting, Doug. You seem to be unhappy with me, for some reason, and you're taking it out on two innocent people."

He was defensive, and his answer didn't make sense. He told me he'd get to the bottom of it. And he told me he had the final authority on all new county hires—which, to me, indicated that he was the bottom of it.

"Joan and John have worked for me and they deserve to be paid, Doug. I hope we can get this settled between the two of us. Otherwise I'll have to bring in the lawyers."

The county prosecutor, John Ladenburg, nipped this little episode in the bud, writing Doug a letter telling him I had the right to hire two staff members, and that he should drop the whole thing. The *News Tribune* picked up the story, and followed it with an editorial titled: "Sutherland: Back Off." The editorial ended with the line: "He should concede that as elected officials, Pearsall-Stipek and Gelman must answer to the voters, not the executive, for the quality of their hiring decisions."

Doug did back off—this time. But he'd made it clear that we were at war. And it felt like a war, every day. It felt like I was back in the trenches, fighting for Joe against pig-headed administrators—but this time I was struggling against a wannabe dictator with delusions of grandeur.

When I got my first look at the office, it looked like a tornado had hit it. The break room looked like it hadn't seen a scrub brush since Nixon was president. John and Joan and I rolled up our sleeves and attacked it—I tackled the sink myself, practically chiseling away a scummy black layer to uncover the stainless steel. Some of the food in the back of the refrigerator looked like it had been there for months.

There was no storage space in the office, so people were piling papers and other things on their desks, or stashing them in boxes underneath their desks. I tried to find the budget, to learn a bit about how the office worked and see what we might do to expand storage—but I couldn't find a budget anywhere. So I hired a gal, Carol, to come in and sort through everything on top of and under the desks, and I ordered a few shelving units for storing what she'd collected. I told my staff they were welcome to keep their stuff on these shelves—but I didn't want any more piles on top of or under desks. I wanted our customers to see that we were an organized, orderly office, on top of things, and ready to help.

The staff didn't seem to like this—or me—very much. From the start, many of the people on staff seemed to resent me for trying to organize things. They'd gotten used to working for Brian, and they didn't like somebody coming in and changing things up. I got the sense that something wasn't quite right, that there was more going on than met the eye.

Turns out, I wasn't just being paranoid. I noticed something strange shortly after taking office: There were three men who worked in the elections department that all had brand-new computers with twenty-two-inch screens. In the back storage area, where I'd had the new shelves installed, there were several other computers, newer models, with eighteen- to twenty-inch screens, just sitting there in storage. While these guys were staring at screens big as billboards, our people in the recording department were sharing ten ancient computers, with screens so small they might as well have been looking through keyholes. How could they even see what they were doing, I wondered?

I guess these guys thought I was born yesterday: They'd ordered their new computers right before the end of the year, and thrown away the boxes as soon as they'd received them so they couldn't be returned—I think they knew enough about me to know I would have them sent back right away.

I didn't want to start an argument, my first days in office, so I let that go. But I did march up to Arthur, one of my elections people, and said: "Those computers in the back? They're going to the recording department."

"I'm sorry, Cathy," he said. "You can't do that. The computers in back are only used during elections."

My hackles went up as soon as I heard "You can't do that," but I was still green enough to wonder if there might be some rule about the computers I didn't know. So I decided to check with Pat Kenny, the budget director.

"They're your computers, Cathy," said Pat. "You can do whatever you want with them."

So I sent the people in the recording department over to elections, to trade their old computers in for the better ones. And I made a mental note not to let my staff tell me what I could and couldn't do.

I'll admit: This whole computer business was still a mystery to me. I didn't understand what all the fuss over computers and screen sizes was about—but I knew it mattered to my staff, so it had to matter to me. Still, seeing everyone glued to those glowing screens all day long was unsettling. I wanted nothing to do with it. If I wanted to communicate with somebody, I had a phone and a typewriter.

The elections guys offered to set me up with my own computer—as a peace offering, maybe—but I told them: "No way. I don't want one of those things. Joan wants one. Give it to her."

It took a while for me to stop swimming against the tide. But I soon realized I was going to need a computer to keep my head above water. I had to bite the bullet and start using one.

But my transition into the Information Age wasn't all smooth sailing. When the IT folks came in to train the staff, they used games to teach them how to operate their machines. Next thing I knew, half the office was "practicing" their computer skills: playing games on the clock. I shut that down pretty quickly.

And then there was Shannon, this new gal I hired. She hadn't been there but a few days when I found an email from her in my inbox. I thought: *What the hell?* I could look out my office door and see her sitting there, a few steps away! It bugged the heck out of me. So I marched up to Shannon's desk and said: "Listen. I don't want you sending me emails. We solve problems face-to-face. If you ever send me another email, you'll be looking for another place to work." The poor thing looked a little shocked, a little bewildered.

Looking back, of course I was fighting a losing battle on that front. But in that office, there were other lines of defense being set up that needed to be knocked down. My first weeks were full of odd little discoveries, each stranger than the next, and I was feeling a little edgy.

To me, the office atmosphere was a little too casual, a little too lenient. I didn't like the way people dressed—some of them looked like they'd taken a wrong turn on their way to the dump. I wanted to say: Garbage and Recycling is down the hall, kids. But instead I announced a new dress code: No jeans except on Fridays. No sweatshirts. No T-shirts. We needed to show our respect for the public we served. They complied, but made it obvious they didn't like it.

In the 1990s, the offices of both the auditor and the assessor-treasurer were in the Pierce County Annex, a former department store on 38th Street. A few blocks away was a warehouse where we kept the voting machines. One day, I paid a visit to the warehouse owner, who occupied the other half of the building. He dropped a bombshell:

"You know what's going on in there, in your part of the warehouse, right?" he said. "Some of the equipment over there isn't voting equipment. You should have a look."

So I walked over to our side of the warehouse. Picture this: A huge space, big enough to park a fleet of buses, with all the county's voting machines laid out in rows, each on its own table, with plenty of space in between, as if they were being set up for an election. It was more room than we probably needed, just to store some machines.

But that wasn't the strange part. In one corner, near the front door, was a full-blown gym, with all kinds of equipment: weight sets, a bench, a stationary bike, a treadmill, and other stuff.

As I was picking my jaw up off the floor, a young fellow appeared—I don't remember where he came from, but I do remember he didn't seem too busy. I asked him his name. He was Jack, he said, and his job was to look after the voting equipment.

"And what about all this equipment?" I asked, nodding at the gym.

"Oh, Brian and I set that up," he said. "We worked out in the mornings. I was kind of his personal trainer."

If that didn't take the cake! These boys pumping iron on the taxpayers' dime! But I didn't want to pick a fight. I bit my tongue.

"Jack," I said, calmly, "I'm going to need for you to come up to the office when we're not in election mode, and work with the rest of the elections staff. I'll see you there tomorrow."

And Jack did show up the next day. But he didn't show up the day after that. Now that he wasn't getting paid to lift weights, I guess he'd lost interest in public service. We never saw Jack again.

One of the first things I did after taking office was check in with the auto licensing people—in Washington, the counties act as service providers for the State Department of Licensing, issuing licenses, plates, and vehicle tabs—and ask if I could order a vanity plate for my car. I wanted it to read "My Way" to recognize how I managed to get things done in Pierce County, and maybe to send a message to this new breed of Big Boys who thought they were going to push me around. I'd cut my teeth on tougher challengers than them. I don't think they understood that I was never going to knuckle under. But they were going to learn.

"My Way" was taken, unfortunately, so one of the staff members suggested changing the spelling to "Mai," like in "Mai

Tai." Luckily, that was available so I swooped it up. As I write this, more than thirty years later, this is still my license plate.

Doug Sutherland had the gall to print up a new official letterhead for the Office of the County Executive, with all the departments—parks, human services, public works, finance, and others—listed beneath him. The list included both me and Barbara Gelman. As if we were his employees!

Not long after he'd lost the payroll battle, he launched another one, corralling me and Barbara into a weekly meeting with all the county department heads. He'd decided that the auditor and assessor-treasurer were "departments" of the county government, and were required to attend these meetings.

And there I was, an elected official, listening to people drone on about garbage pickups and parking meters. I sat through one of these marathon sessions, wasting an entire morning. My office was the busiest and most public facing in the county. We served people all day long, from the moment we opened our door every morning. So by the time that first department meeting was finally winding down, I was squirming in my seat, anxious to get back to doing real work.

After it was over, I approached him and said: "Doug, why am I here? I have people at my door. I can't spend all morning listening to stuff that has nothing to do with me."

"Sorry," he said, "but I need to know what's happening in all my departments."

"Well, if you need to know what I'm doing, I'll let you know. But I'm not coming to your meetings."

"I'll come to you, then."

He tried this a couple of times. He came to my office early, to poke around and ask questions that didn't have anything to do with his office. I don't think he was really interested in what I was doing. He was just trying to pretend he was my boss. But these "meetings" never went very far. Before we'd even start, somebody would come into the office and interrupt, needing this or that. There were no quiet mornings at the auditor's office.

So Doug abandoned his weekly show of dominance, because it made him look silly. But he was only beginning to make my life difficult.

And he wasn't the only one. In February, I learned that Brian Sonntag—for reasons I honestly don't understand, to this day—considered me an enemy. I hadn't been in office a month—and neither had he, as Washington State Auditor—when I got a call from his office in Olympia, saying they were going to audit my office.

What on Earth did they think they were going to find? I was working with the same people who'd worked with Brian. The only things I'd changed so far were the computers and the dress code. When the printing department called, asking if I wanted to change any of the forms, I told them just to replace Brian's name with mine and leave it at that. So why would Brian send one of his people to Tacoma to poke around my office?

The audit itself was strange. When Brian's man showed up, I greeted him politely and told him I would do whatever I could to help him do his job. He thanked me and said, "I'll start with the elections department."

"Now hold on," I said. "Elections are the Secretary of State's business. Your office has nothing to do with them. You can look at all our financials, but the election department's records are off limits."

He didn't really seem to have much interest in my financial records. He left soon afterward.

This whole situation bothered me, and I thought about it for a long time afterward. I'd been a dedicated public servant for nearly twenty years. I'd conducted many campaigns, from the local to the federal level. But I still had a lot to learn about the nuts and bolts of running elections, keeping public records, granting and recording marriage licenses—all my new responsibilities. I assumed my staff would be eager to help. But I couldn't even find the budget for the office! Nobody would admit to having anything to do with it, so I had to hunt it down myself. Nobody wanted to share any information with me. From the start, there had been a kind of resistance, an unspoken attitude of "You're so smart, you figure it out." And I did figure it out. It just took much longer than it needed to. Why were they all trying to keep me in the dark?

It was clear by now that some of them were in constant contact with Brian. It was tiring, and irritating, to hear them say "You can't do that" every time I asked them to do something differently. Who was telling them what I could and couldn't do?

My appointment was for just one year, with an election coming up in the 1993 September primary for the remainder of the term. After that, we'd be back on track with regular four-year terms, beginning with the 1994 general election. I liked the job, and I wanted to keep it, so I launched a bid for the 1993 election. But campaigning wasn't my top priority. There were other things I wanted to accomplish.

We hit the ground running that first year. One of the first things I wanted to tackle was voter education. I had this idea to create an informational pamphlet that would explain ballot measures and candidate positions.

It may seem like a common-sense idea, but back then only the State of Washington was publishing informational pamphlets for Pierce County voters—and only for the general elections. I took the idea to the County Council, and they agreed to let me do it just this first time, to see how it went. It was no walk in the park: Because each taxing district paid for their own elections, I had to go to each city, each fire district, each water district, etc. to get their approval on the pamphlet and its wording.

But all that legwork paid off. The voters ate it up. And once they'd seen that first pamphlet, they wanted one for every election. The pamphlet became a fixture in Pierce County elections.

These were my main goals as auditor: To get as many people voting as possible, to make it as easy as possible for everyone to vote, and to make elections as secure as possible. We spent hours out among the public—I spent hours myself, at a table I set up at the entrances of grocery stores—registering new voters. We sent staff to every high school in the county with sample voting machines and mail-in ballots, to show them how it all worked.

Back then, not too many people were absentee voters— about 15,000, county-wide—but the Republican Secretary of State, Ralph Munro, had pushed through a law making it easier: Once you signed up to receive an absentee ballot, you'd get one automatically for all future elections.

The envelopes containing these absentee ballots weren't exactly user-friendly, though. They weren't easy to open without damaging the contents, and it wasn't clear where to sign the return envelope—and an unsigned envelope meant an invalid ballot. So while we shopped around for better envelopes, we also hosted sessions where new voters could learn how to use them.

But despite all our accomplishments, I couldn't shake the feeling that not everybody in the office was pulling in the same direction. Some staff were talking to people outside the office, including the press. This is just one example: When I attended a national conference of county election officials in Phoenix, Arizona, to learn about new ballot processing technologies, I took Dave along, spending a couple of vacation days in Las Vegas on the way back. Not long after, the Pierce County Herald published an editorial cartoon depicting me as some kind of madwoman at a casino, frantically pumping coins into a slot machine. I couldn't figure out the point of it. More importantly: how did a cartoonist know Dave and I had stopped in Las Vegas?

Cartoon by Chris Washburn

Sometime in the spring of 1993, I received a notice to appear before the Washington State Public Disclosure Commission, to answer charges in a complaint filed by one of my constituents: a man by the name of Dale Washam.

I'd only recently heard of Dale Washam, because he'd filed to run against me in the fall, for the one-year unexpired term. Now, Dale was a character. He was a friend of Brian Sonntag, and seemed to make a career of legal battles, often representing himself, armed with an associate degree in arts and sciences from Fort Steilacoom Community College. How he made his living was a mystery: He hadn't had a paying job since 1980, when he'd been fired for doing sketchy things as a pharmaceutical salesman.

Dale Washam's main charge against me was that I'd been illegally promoting my campaign for auditor by having my name printed on official materials like ballots and return envelopes. I was surprised by the accusation. I'd simply told the print shop to just replace Brian Sonntag's name with mine on all the auditor's documents and stationery.

Fortunately, a woman named Sally Andrews, who printed ballots and other materials for many of the state's auditors, got wind of this, and offered to come with me to the hearing. She explained to the commission that her other auditor clients did the exact same thing: Their names were printed on all the ballots and official envelopes. The commission dismissed the charge.

It was my first victory against Dale Washam, but it wouldn't be the last. He kept coming for me. He became a major thorn in my side, a Big Boy who would spend the next decade trying to attack and undermine me. I never really thought of him as an opponent, though—more of an irritant. He was the most annoying person I think I'd ever dealt with. He was one of those people who, when you looked at his past, seemed to be trying to punish other people for all his misdeeds.

Luckily, it turned out the campaign to serve as auditor through 1994 wasn't a hard one. I beat Dale Washam by more than nine points, and was elected to serve another year as Pierce County Auditor.

I got a call right after the election from Bill Baarsma, the chair of the Pierce County Democrats. "Cathy," he said, "what did you do?"

I was taken aback. "What do you mean?"

Bill wanted to know how it could have happened that one of the party's chosen candidates for port commissioner—one of five commissioners who oversaw the operation and management of the Port of Tacoma—had lost his reelection bid. The candidate's name was Phil Lelli, and he'd been a popular commissioner; by all accounts a good guy, a former longshoreman and union leader who'd been a labor advocate for more than twenty years. I was familiar with his face, because he'd put up campaign billboards all over town with his picture on them, and I'd thought to myself: *I wouldn't have used that picture. He looks like a criminal. Like a Mafia hit man.*

Mr. Lelli had lost by almost twelve points, so I told Bill I didn't think there was much chance anything had gone sideways with the vote tally.

"But could you do a hand recount anyway?" he asked.

"Tell you what, Bill," I said. "We'll pull a few hundred ballots at random from six districts, and we'll recount them by hand."

That seemed to satisfy him. When we finished our hand recount, not a single vote differed from our machine count. Bill was surprised his candidate had lost—but he knew the election had been fair and well-run.

He wouldn't be the only one to suspect shenanigans when a Pierce County election didn't go his way, though. It was a call I would receive many times after elections over the next nine years: "Cathy, what did you do?"

❧

Just weeks before that November general election, we faced another challenge. Mike, from the election staff, came to my office with a box full of cards, printed in red ink: requests for absentee ballots, all of them from Republican voters in the county. The State Republican Party had sent these out to encourage mail-in voting, to take advantage of the new state law.

There were two tax-related state initiatives on the ballot that fall, both aimed at limiting taxes and spending. The Republican Party was pushing to get them passed—even though a former Republican governor and U.S. Senator, Daniel J. Evans, had spoken out against them.

My staff and I had to shift into another gear. By law, all ballots had to be mailed out to voters no later than eighteen days before an election. I had to hire new staff to enter all these new voters' information into the system and order more mail-in ballots. It was a scramble, but we got it done.

The election results were mixed: One tax initiative narrowly passed, and the other was defeated. But the election presented a new problem: Almost overnight, the term "absentee ballot" was obsolete—these new voters weren't absentees. They all lived and voted in Pierce County. And the number of people who voted by mail in Pierce County had doubled, from 15,000 to 30,000.

My staff told me that in previous elections, they'd process absentee ballots at their desks each day—opening them, verifying them, and scanning them—and then lock them in a secure room at night where they'd wait to be tallied. State law prohibited tallying the votes until after the polls closed on Election Day.

The sudden shift in how people were voting made it necessary to rethink this entire process. It was clear that elections were changing, and that we would need to change with it. As we processed this new batch of mail-in ballots, it was obvious we needed more space. And the only space I could find, given the time crunch, was in the break room—but we all knew this was just a temporary fix.

In the meantime, I knew I had to do something about my election staff. Some were starting to act up—maybe they thought they smelled blood in the water, because a couple of negative articles had run in the newspaper. With all the changes I was implementing—the new voter pamphlets, outreach programs, new ballot-handling procedures—I was asking them to do things they hadn't done before, and some of them pushed back, saying: "Sorry, that's not in my job description. You can't require me to do that."

"You can't." I was so damned tired of hearing that! So I went to the county's HR department, and told them I was going to rewrite some job descriptions.

And do you know what they said? *"You can't do that."*

Turns out, I really couldn't do that. It was government policy: An employer couldn't change someone's job requirements after they'd been hired.

So I asked them: "What can I do, then?"

The only solution that was legally defensible, they said, was to fire everyone on the staff, rewrite the job descriptions, and let them reapply.

I felt terrible, but I felt I had no choice. I needed a team that was willing to adapt and grow with the changes we were facing in the auditor's office. So I fired every single staff member at the end of the year, and invited them to reapply for their jobs in the coming term.

CHAPTER 12

Ballots, Not Bricks

(1994)

I **DIDN'T LIKE FIRING PEOPLE.** I tried to sugar-coat it when I let my staff go at the end of 1993: It was really just a formality, I said, an on-the-level way to update their job descriptions. They'd be first in line for their jobs when they reapplied.

And I did hire all of them back—all but one, who didn't reapply; I guess he decided he'd had enough of me. The rest seemed pretty darn grateful to get their jobs back, which was strange—they were working the same jobs, some of them with even more on their plates. But I think getting the boot, even if it was just to check a box for the bureaucrats, had scared some of them straight.

It was like day and night with the staff after that. It might have had something to do with the fact that they couldn't dismiss me as the unelected upstart who'd taken Brian Sonntag's place. The people had spoken, electing me to do what I said I'd do: get more folks voting, and make it easier and more secure to cast a ballot. And I had kept my promise to them, to let them have their old—if slightly tweaked—jobs back.

From that point on, things were different. We were allies now, a team working together to achieve those goals.

There was still a thorn in my side, though. I'd inherited an urgent problem: The computerized system being used to store and retrieve records like deeds, liens, and powers of attorney was so outdated that it often crashed. It drove the people in the Recording Department up the wall, and sometimes got them in trouble with impatient constituents. Before I'd even arrived, the county had charged some apparent genius in the IT department with designing a new recording system. He'd formed a committee with people in King and Snohomish Counties, who were in the same boat.

I'd sent John, my deputy, to work with this committee, but let me tell you, it was like my county council days all over again: meeting after meeting, week after week, and not a damned thing to show for it.

I was starting to get frustrated with John. It wasn't long after I'd brought him on board that I realized he was going to be a handful. He was one of the most intelligent people I'd ever met, but he wasn't people-smart: He was arrogant, cocky, a little high-handed with people in the office. I did my best to run interference between him and the staff—it was supposed to be his job to be a buffer for me, but I had to play the hand I'd dealt myself—and we'd managed, mostly. But he was always stirring up trouble. He liked to shoot his mouth off to reporters without thinking, which was always good for a few laughs—but I never saw the funny side. I was forever cleaning up his messes, for the press and for our higher-ups.

During my second year as auditor, John played a leading role in a mess that took years to resolve. Apparently one of our employees had complained to the public employees' union that she was being harassed and bullied by her supervisors—mostly by John. John got wind of it, and when a piece of mail from the union arrived in the office, addressed to her, he took it upon himself to open it and see what the clerk and the union were up to. I think we probably could have resolved her complaint without much fuss, until he did that. The employee quit, sued, and was later awarded a judgement so huge it shocked everyone, until a judge finally reduced it on appeal.

Not long after this, we learned John was not only a loose cannon—he was also a bit of a sex addict. We'd just handed out government cell phones to key staff members, including John, and after the first bill rolled in, our budget gal, Lori, approached me and said, "Cathy, you should see this. John's phone bill is off the charts." There were hundreds of calls, mostly to the same two or three numbers. The bill was staggering.

I was really steamed. "Find out who those numbers belong to," I said. "I want to know who he's been calling."

They were phone sex lines. John was using taxpayer money to get his jollies with strangers over the phone.

I knew I had to get in front of this one with Doug Sutherland, who I figured would hit the roof when he found out. I didn't want him thinking I was trying to sweep it under the rug. So I went to see him, and told him all about John, and he didn't bat an eyelash. He must have already heard about it. His reaction made me wonder what other skeletons he'd had to stuff into the county's closet. I told John I was on to him, and that there would be no taxpayer-funded sex games. He seemed to stay out of trouble, mostly, after that.

I knew the job of auditor involved a lot of work that I'd never done before, and not long after I'd taken office, I joined an organization that would allow me to bounce ideas off other people in my position, from all over the country: The National Association of County Recorders, Election Officials and Clerks, which went by the acronym NACRC. Everyone pronounces it "nackrack." As the name indicated, its members were concerned with every part of my job.

NACRC had an annual conference, every March, in Washington, D.C. I had always been close with my grandkids, but it was around this time, the early 1990s, that we became even closer. I realized this trip to the nation's capital was an opportunity to teach the kids about their country and its history. I couldn't take all of them with me in one trip, of course, so Dave and I took one at a time. While I met with the NACRC, Dave showed each kid around. They'd visit the White House, the Smithsonian, Monticello, Arlington National Cemetery, the Capitol, and other places. We introduced them to members of Congress, took them to meet Norm Dicks and his wife at his office. And if it was a Pearsall grandchild, we would stop in Bloomfield, Indiana, to visit my mother's family farm on our way home, to reconnect them with their Feutz and Emery relatives.

These were also the years that Joe and Jill's marriage started to come apart. They separated and eventually divorced, splitting custody evenly, every other week. Joe worked hard at his job—and at one point Jill was working two jobs, just to stay afloat. They both needed a lot of help during those years. The girls, especially Justine and Jaclyn, spent a lot of time with me and Dave. Every other weekend, we picked them up from Jill's place and brought them to our home. Dave drove the girls to and from school, and they ate a lot of their meals with us. They even joined us for our vacations, to Hawaii and Palm Springs. Dave loved Palm Springs, so much that in later years, after our work schedules had slowed down a bit, we talked about buying a second home there. But I told Dave I couldn't do it. I couldn't spend that much time away from the grandchildren.

At one of these NACRC conferences, I met a man whose company had developed a recording system that sounded like just the upgrade our office needed: a stable, searchable database of public records. So I asked him to pay me a visit and give me his pitch and a bid, which he did—and I was so impressed with what his system could do that I told John and the committee I was going a different way. The people from King and Snohomish Counties, once they got wind of this new system, snapped it up. Officials from each county scheduled their install for March of 1994.

That rubbed me the wrong way. It had been my idea in the first place, and here they were, cutting the line. I wasn't about to let that fly—if they had theirs installed first, it would take ages for ours to get done. I ran it by Doug Sutherland, who wasn't crazy about the extra expense, but there was no denying we needed a new system yesterday, and this was the only workable idea anyone had managed to come up with. He gave it the green light.

But talking with the contractor, I realized we were in for more than replacing just the system itself. We needed new equipment—connecting cables, computers, even deeper countertops—to make it all work. I had my own people run the numbers, and it looked like we would need about $300,000 to get it all done.

I took the estimate to Pat Kenny, but he shot it down: "You can't do that." Not enough funds available in the county budget, he said. So I fired back: "Well, what if I manage to trim $300,000 out of my own budget?"

He laughed. "Cathy, if you can pull that off, you can do the office remodel."

I had a pretty good idea where to start swinging the ax: When I first took over, I noticed some of the staff treating the place like a twenty-four-hour diner. Recording folks would roll in on Saturdays for half-days, and a couple of elections guys were racking up overtime pay, time-and-a-half, working extra days. That was my first big slash, putting the kibosh on any hours over the standard forty-hour week. They would have to get their work done from Monday to Friday. As you can imagine, this didn't score me many points with the staff.

I found other ways to cut. Instead of hiring part-timers for election rushes, for example, I began recruiting Election Day volunteers among local community groups—a tactic I would use even more down the road. This saved more money than I'd anticipated, and within just a few months I had squirreled away that $300,000, and Pat told me I could spend it. I ordered the remodel, and I ordered the new recording system. And just to stick it to King and Snohomish Counties, I scheduled the install for President's Day weekend in February—a month before they would get theirs.

It was a huge relief for my staff, and for anyone in Pierce County who needed access to their official records. Even Doug Sutherland seemed happy—or at least hadn't found anything to complain about.

But if anyone thought this was the start of a beautiful friendship between me and the county executive, they had another think coming. After we'd spruced up the place and installed the new recording system, I noticed the newly painted walls seemed kind of bare. It took me a few months to get around to it, but I ordered about a half-dozen inspirational pictures to hang on the walls, to brighten up the place.

About a week after we'd hung them up, I got a call from Pat.

"Cathy," he said, "did you buy some pictures for your office?"

"Yeah," I said. I was surprised he thought it worth mentioning. "I bought pictures."

"I'm sorry. Doug wants you to send those back. He doesn't think you should have bought them. He thinks they're an unnecessary expense."

I didn't bother asking Pat who was reporting the details of my office supply purchases to the county executive. I wasn't sure I wanted to know.

"Tell you what, Pat," I said. "I'm not taking them down or

sending them back. If it's such a big deal to Doug, he can come down and do it. I've got the receipts right here."

He was quiet for a moment. Finally, he said, "I'll see what I can do."

I never heard another peep about the pictures. Did Doug really care about them? I doubt it. I think he was just sore that I'd scored a big win for the public and managed to rustle up that $300,000 he wouldn't release to me. And I think he just wanted to see if he could make me jump through a little hoop for him.

He still hadn't figured out who he was dealing with.

Those first few weeks of the 1994 term, my staff and I were up to our eyeballs getting ready for a special election in early February, which included thirty-five funding measures for the county's school districts.

Now, school tax levies and bonds in Washington State weren't decided by simple majority votes. The state constitution had two requirements for their passage: First, at least 40 percent of the folks who voted in the last general election needed to vote on a measure. And second, at least 60 percent of those voters needed to vote "yes." Even with those hurdles, these school tax levies usually sailed through. People wanted to support their local schools.

The special election results knocked us for a loop: Only nine of the thirty-five school levy propositions passed. Nobody had ever seen anything like it. One of the initiatives was a $54 million bond that would have funded the building of a new school in the overcrowded Tacoma Public School District—a no-brainer, everyone thought; a sure thing. But the bond measure fell just short, with 59.84 percent of voters supporting it. Of course, I got a call from the Tacoma Public Schools superintendent, Rudy Crew. He was furious.

"Cathy," he barked, "what did you do?"

The game-changer in this election was those mail-in ballots. In the past, absentee ballots usually made up most of the "yes" votes that had put these school initiatives over the top. But the Republican drive to get their voters signed up for automatic mail-in ballots had paid off, significantly boosting Republican turnout. We'd seen a bit of that in November, in the strange results on the tax measures. But this time? They came out of the woodwork for a special election most of them would have just ignored before. And let's face it, Republicans aren't known for their tendency to vote for new taxes and bonds.

It hit me like a ton of bricks: If vote-by-mail wasn't available to everyone, it could be used as a tool to subvert the people's will. It had been years since we'd seen a school bond go down in flames, and now suddenly three-fourths of them were toast. It was obvious that mail-in ballots were going to make up a bigger slice of the pie in every election on the horizon. And so my staff and I began to put together a plan to ensure they were increased across the board, to grow the electorate and level the playing field.

The plan had a few moving parts. First, we needed to spread the work about the new law. A lot of people still weren't aware they could be permanent vote-by-mail voters, receiving ballots for every election automatically. Previously, anyone who wanted an absentee ballot had to request one for every election.

Second, I looked at the numbers from our hundreds of polling stations all over Pierce County. Unless it were a presidential election, most of these places were ghost towns. For off-year special elections, some only saw two or three voters all day. So here we were, paying people to staff these polling stations where only a handful were going to show up.

This was some low-hanging fruit. I saw a way to expand vote-by-mail, with the additional benefit of cutting costs for the county: I started closing each polling station where fewer than ten people voted. Then I fired off letters to voters in those precincts, giving them the heads-up about the closures and letting them know they were now permanent vote-by-mail voters.

I knew I was in for some blowback—people don't like change—but even I was caught off guard by the firestorm that followed. The complaints came at me from all angles. People were bent out of shape about losing the "tradition" of moseying down to the polling place on Election Day, casting their vote, and then shooting the breeze with their friends and neighbors over cookies and coffee.

I kept my mouth shut, but I thought: What friends and neighbors? I was only shutting down places that saw fewer than ten people. Two or three people munching on cookies seemed like a waste of resources to me.

I remember one woman complaining—I think in a letter to the newspaper —that having her ballot mailed to her home made her worry that her husband would try to tell her how to vote. I ignored that one. It was too silly to respond to. If your husband is telling you how to vote, you've got bigger problems.

The one charge I took seriously was that voters were having a choice taken from them, the choice between voting in person and voting by mail. But I had a hunch this was just a fear of something new and better—we weren't taking away their voting privilege; we were just making it a walk in the park. And I suspected that once they took advantage of this new option, they wouldn't want to go back to the old way of doing things. And time would prove me right.

For now, though, the decision had brought out all the crazies, with their wild accusations and conspiracy theories about how vote-by-mail was going to open the floodgates for all kinds of skullduggery and corruption. There were concerns about security, but they were all misguided. Still, critics were watching us like hawks—and some of those critics were in cahoots with Dale Washam.

In April, Dale Washam slapped me with a lawsuit, accusing me and my election staff of feeding mail-in ballots into vote-tallying machines before Election Day. Now, state law said we could organize absentee ballots beginning ten days before an election, and we scanned the ballots in advance. But they weren't counted until after the polls closed on Election Day. Everything we did was by the book, and we had a paper trail a mile long to prove it.

In his lawsuit, Washam implied that having ballots opened before the election would invite workers to peek and make mental tallies of the vote totals—like counting cards at a casino. It was ridiculous. For the upcoming general election, we had eighty-five different types of mail-in ballots going out to voters. And staff were being watched continuously during the day.

To the *News Tribune*, Washam claimed his lawsuit was about "what's right and what's wrong," but I smelled a rat: He'd filed to run for Pierce County Auditor again in the fall, and the lawsuit and the press coverage gave him what amounted to a free attack ad against me.

I'll give you this: the laws and regulations about how to handle and process mail-in ballots weren't as clear as they needed to be, especially now that the number—and percentage—of mail-in voters was growing so fast. But I also think many of the laws and regulations to come were more about preventing the appearance of funny business with the ballots rather than making any real changes. Because we were playing by the rules already on the books, Dale Washam's lawsuit was ultimately dismissed—but not until after the November election.

Part of the reason my staff and I were working so hard to get mail-in ballots scanned before Election Day was because they were a nightmare to process: Each ballot came back in a sealed return envelope with a signature we had to match to the voter's registration record. Inside that was a "secrecy sleeve"—another envelope, sealed tightly for privacy—containing the actual ballot. Both were a bear to open, and we had to handle them with kid gloves: A tear or kink anywhere on the ballot could prevent it from being scanned completely.

I had three full-time election department staff, and of course had to hire temporary help to handle the avalanche. These mail-in ballots—which had already doubled in number from 15,000 to 30,000, and were likely to double again before the fall—had to be opened, verified, opened again, and scanned for later tallying. Over time, this felt like torture. The seconds my staff spent struggling with the envelopes might not seem like much, but they added up. Consider this: If a person could verify a voter's signature, open the envelope and inner security sleeve, and scan a ballot, all in ten seconds, it would still take that person more than eighty-three hours to process 30,000 of them.

So I needed a few things, right away. First, more bodies. People cost money, and hiring part-time help was expensive, but it was the only way to keep our heads above water for now. Where I could, I enlisted the help of volunteers.

I also needed more room to process and securely store the ballots before the count. Cordoning off half the break room and locking the doors wasn't enough, and surely wouldn't be enough as the number of mail-in voters continued to grow. I began by looking for space within the annex, and found it: An abandoned print shop that nobody was using for printing anymore. People all over the building had been using it as a big junk drawer instead, packed with things they didn't want to throw out, even though they weren't using them, and boxes that looked like they hadn't been touched in years. It was a mess.

I asked Doug if I could repurpose the room for secure ballot processing, and he gave me the go-ahead. I put out a notice to everyone in the building: Come get your stuff out of the old print shop, or it's heading to the dump. I gave them a reasonable deadline, and told them anything in the shop after that would be thrown out. I think my reputation preceded me, because boy, did they get that stuff out of there fast. Once they'd cleaned it out, I had it painted and we moved our people and equipment in. It was a huge deal, moving the ballots out of the office and off people's desks. While we'd always taken every precaution and followed the law to a T, I'll admit it all looked a little chaotic. It was nice to have everything election-related locked down in a secure location.

The third problem I needed to solve was the envelopes. They were really something, and they were slowing us down and bleeding us dry with labor costs, literally adding dozens of staff-hours. I reached out to other county auditors across the state for envelope samples, but only a handful bothered to respond.

So I wasn't getting much help with the envelope headache, not yet. I would need more time to figure that one out—and to have more time, I needed to win a full term in office in November of 1994.

There was a fourth problem, too, one that I knew would be a long-term fight: A large enough group of people, including some opinion-shapers in Pierce County, remained skeptical of vote-by mail. The cartoonists for Pierce County newspapers had long had their eye on me—to them I was quite a character, a rich source of material, and an easy target. But I often struggled to understand what these cartoonists were aiming at. Sometime after Chris Washburn, the Pierce County Herald cartoonist, drew me as a deranged gambler in Las Vegas, the cartoonist for Peninsula Gateway, the Gig Harbor paper, Don Snowden, published a cartoon that I think he meant as an attack on mail-in voting. He drew a long line of voters, stretching back over the countryside for about a mile, waiting for their turn to enter a lone voting booth on top of a hill. A sign over the booth was labeled "Absentee Only."

What? The whole point of mail-in voting was to avoid lines altogether. I still don't get the point of that one.

I was set to go toe-to-toe against Dale Washam again, and I wasn't really losing much sleep over it. Nobody else had filed to run for auditor as the deadline approached, and during the week of filing in May, I made a point to greet the new candidates as they came in, to get to know them and answer any questions they might have. At closing time on Friday, around 4:30, I told the election staff to lock the doors and close up. I remember heading up to my office and heaving a little sigh of relief, thinking: *This is great. I won't have anyone running against me in the primary.*

It was maybe five minutes later when one of the election staff members came knocking on my door.

"Cathy," she said, "there are two women filing papers for their candidacy. They showed up right before the deadline. You want to handle it?"

I went down and saw two gals I'd never laid eyes on before.

"Hello," I said. "And what office are you here to file for?"

"Auditor." She said it cool as a cucumber—almost like she didn't realize she was saying it to the person she'd be squaring off against.

I was a bit shocked. Wasn't expecting that one! But I played it cool, like it was just another day in the office. "Okay," I said. I gave her the paperwork, explained what I could, and told her to let me know if she had any questions. Then I turned to the other woman, who'd been silent.

"And what can I do for you?" I said.

"I'm with her."

They filled out the forms and left. As I was filing, I caught the new candidate's name: Jacqueline Hyde. I'd seen the name in the news recently: Jacquie Hyde was the widow of Tacoma's mayor, Jack Hyde, who had died of a heart attack in January after serving only seventeen days in office. Someone on the staff recognized the woman with Jacquie as T.K.K., a political mover and shaker who'd been a union rabble-rouser. Apparently, she was now Jacquie's campaign manager.

Jacquie Hyde had never run for office before, and she didn't seem like a political animal. I wondered: Who had put her up to this? Who was pulling the strings?

It didn't take long for me to figure it out. A short time later, I got a call from Connie Ladenburg, the wife of our county prosecutor, John Ladenburg, who was running for prosecuting attorney. Connie thought John and I might join forces and run a tag-team campaign, since neither of us expected much competition. When she came by that evening, we sat out in the pool house and I told her I was no longer running unopposed in the primary. This was news to Connie. We were still talking about it, and how it might throw a wrench into our joint campaign, when the phone rang. It was a reporter from the *News Tribune*.

"Ms. Pearsall-Stipek, why did you throw a brick through Jacquie Hyde's window?"

I honestly couldn't speak for a second. "What?" I said. "I didn't throw a brick through anyone's window."

"Did your deputy, John Gamble?"

"I'm sorry, sir, but I don't know what in the world you are talking about."

He hung up.

I don't remember what Connie said in those next few minutes after I'd told her I'd just been accused of throwing a brick through my opponent's window. But I remember she didn't stick around long. And that was the last I heard about running a joint campaign with John.

The next morning, when I went into the office, there was reporter from the Seattle Times waiting to pounce on me.

"Ms. Pearsall-Stipek, I'm here because you threw a brick through Jacquie Hyde's window."

I did my best to sound cool and professional, but I was getting peeved. "Do I look like I could throw a brick through a window?" I said. "I mean, good God. If you'd ever seen me throw anything, you'd know how ridiculous that is." I invited him outside to talk about the campaign if he wanted—we weren't allowed to talk politics on government property. The interview only lasted a few minutes. All he wanted to know was whether someone from our campaign had thrown the brick.

I was completely disgusted. It was such a stupid question. Who in their right mind would go after their political rival in such a ham-fisted, public way? It was like something out of a bad gangster movie.

This was the story that appeared in the *News Tribune*: Earlier in the day, Jacquie Hyde had received a threatening note in her mailbox. She and T.K.K.—they were joined at the hip now, I guess—immediately went to the police station to report it. When she arrived home at about 8:00 p.m., she found a brick on the kitchen counter, under a broken bay window. Attached to the brick was another note that said: "Withdraw or You're Dead."

This is the line from the article that stuck with me: "Police believe the window was broken first and the brick placed inside the window above the kitchen sink."

So nobody had thrown a brick. They'd placed it. Why? It was so dumb. They'd assumed the only possible result would be a flood of outrage and support for Jacquie Hyde, and scorn and criticism for her opponent—me. And when I started to think about it that way, it made a crazy kind of sense. The *News Tribune* quoted Tim Strege, the Young Democrat from South Tacoma who'd become my adversary after I lost my 1972 campaign for the legislature, and who was Jacquie Hyde's good friend. Tim said he was "dismayed." Dennis Flannigan, my friend-turned-nemesis on the County Council, said, "I don't understand someone who would embarrass the human race with such vitriol and such trash." I didn't understand it, either. But the *News Tribune* had drummed up the outrage it was after.

I'm not sure what Jacquie Hyde was playing at. She quit the race, claiming she was scared for her life, and then six days later, she changed her mind—or someone changed her mind for her—and talked a Superior Court judge into letting her back in. After seeing the names Strege and Flannigan in the news article, I had a good idea who was behind her primary challenge.

I had no answers about the brick, and I kept my focus on my campaign. In Pierce County, one of the big events in any candidate's campaign is their interview with the Municipal League of Tacoma-Pierce County. You park yourself in front of an evaluation team and answer questions about your know-how, effectiveness, character, and community involvement. The team also does some digging into your background and checks your references.

The Municipal League was on the other side of town, North Tacoma. When Dave and I drove to the interview, I started to feel a little unnerved: All over town there were huge balloons hovering over the buildings and parking lots, emblazoned with the words: *Vote Jacquie Hyde for Auditor.* Who in their right mind ran for auditor this way? What was going on?

I had a bad feeling in my gut about the interview with the Municipal League team too. Just a couple of weeks back, I'd been accused of pitching a brick at my opponent's house. And I did receive a frosty reception from the evaluation team. There wasn't any laughing or joking. No small talk. The interview was all business. And then I was on my way.

Our friends John and Pat McCarthy lived in North Tacoma, and we hadn't seen them in a while. So Dave and I drove to their place after the interview. Of course, we talked a little about the campaign.

"I have something interesting to tell you, Cathy," John said. And he told me something I'd never heard before: On the night the brick magically appeared on Jacquie Hyde's kitchen counter, he'd gotten a call from Tim Strege. "Tim told me he was over at Jacquie Hyde's house, and somebody had thrown a brick through her window."

Didn't that just beat all? The *News Tribune* hadn't mentioned Tim Strege being there.

"Why would he call you and tell you that?" I asked.

"I think because we're friends." Strege was acting strange, John said. He couldn't put his finger on anything specific Tim said—but he definitely got the feeling Tim wanted John to share the news. That way I wouldn't seem surprised when a reporter asked me about it—which would make me seem guilty.

I can't prove it—and I don't really care anymore—but I think the whole thing was staged. I mean, honestly, who would be dumb enough to pull a stunt like that? Definitely not me.

So I understood why John hadn't given me the heads-up. Pat had always said it: South Tacoma politics were wild, full of shenanigans. It was practically a blood sport. They liked to stay neutral on the North Side, she said. She called the North Side "Switzerland."

A week or two later, the Municipal League's candidate ratings were released: They were never ones to hand out gold stars, but they rarely slapped anyone with the rating they gave Jacquie Hyde: not acceptable. It was their lowest possible rating. Turns out, one of her old colleagues had some things to say about her, and they weren't exactly singing her praises.

Jacquie and her puppet master must have been furious. They complained loudly and repeatedly to the *News Tribune*. T.K.K. called it "the latest brick through the window" of Jacquie's campaign. She managed to get that quote in the paper three times. Boy, were they milking that brick for all it was worth!

So of course, Jacquie sued the Municipal League, which caused at least one local cartoonist to make her, and not me for once, a subject of ridicule. Chris Britt, of the *News Tribune*, drew a cartoon captioned "One Brick Shy. . ." It depicted Jacquie Hyde holding two bricks—one labeled "Paranoia," the other labeled "Frivolous Lawsuits." She'd apparently dropped a third brick, labeled "Political Savvy," that lay on the ground next to her. I guess I wasn't the only one who thought her campaign was a mess.

Cartoon by Chris Britt.
Reprinted with permission

So while Jacquie Hyde was suing the Municipal League, Dale Washam was still suing me. I didn't have anybody to sue, so I did my job while Dave and the other staff ran my campaign. The September primary and the November general were going to be harder to process than the last election. More people would be voting by mail in Pierce County than ever before. We were bracing for 50,000 mail-in ballot requests.

Amid all the drama, the *News Tribune* endorsed me the week before the September primary. The editors wrote that Jacquie Hyde was a "sympathetic figure," but she didn't have the chops or record to qualify. I, on the other hand, could, "legitimately claim credit for effectively reorganizing the office, drastically cutting overtime costs, modernizing the auditor's record-keeping system and speeding election-night vote return." I had also, they noted, boosted voter rolls by 13 percent.

At last! Somebody noticed the good work I was doing.

I sailed past Jacquie Hyde in the September primary like she was standing still, and I handed Dale Washam his hat again in November. I had finally won a four-year term as Pierce County Auditor. And there was a lot of work yet to do.

CHAPTER 13

Mail In Ballots: Changing the Way Washington Votes

(1995–1997)

THE NUMBER OF PERMANENT mail-in voters was sky-rocketing in Pierce County, and we were up to our necks in the auditor's office. I was on good terms with most of the other auditors in the state, but none of them was chomping at the bit to see mail-in voting become the norm in their jurisdictions. It was around this time that I joined another national organization that would allow me to bounce ideas off other people in my position, from all over the country. NACRC was an incredibly helpful organization, but I needed more. It was time to join the Election Center. Also known as the National Association of Election Officials, it's a nonprofit that trains and certifies people to run elections and register voters. Its members, almost all of them government officials from city to state levels, were zeroed in on the new curveballs the job was throwing our way.

I wanted to be armed with the best, most up-to-date information available, because voting by mail had plenty of nay-sayers—and it was fair to say there were still some bugs to be worked out.

Another beef with voting by mail was that it amounted to a

poll tax: At the time, neither the state nor the county was paying the return postage for mail-in ballots, and the oversized return envelopes cost 54 cents each to mail. And voters weren't happy about it. So I thought it was even more urgent to make the materials that went out to them—the envelopes, ballots, and secrecy sleeves—as light and easy to use as possible, and as economical as they could be for my staff to handle. It wouldn't be until 2019 that the Washington State Legislature passed, and Governor Jay Inslee signed, a law requiring all return envelopes for election ballots to be marked postage paid. And there are still only nineteen states—and the District of Columbia—doing their voters the same courtesy.

So I put together a team to work on the envelope issue: my office; the local U.S. Post Office; Griffin Envelope Company; and Uarco, a company that made and printed business and official forms, including ballots and tabbed envelopes like the secrecy sleeves. We all put our heads together to design a better package of materials to ship out to voters.

It wasn't long before the people at the local Post Office and I understood they didn't have the know-how to advise me about changing the mailings. So I called the U.S. congressional representative for our district: Norm Dicks, the man who'd threatened to sink my career in 1978. We'd since buried the hatchet—such is the way of politics—and I asked Norm to hook me up with somebody at the U.S. Postal Service. Norm arranged a meeting in the nation's capital with someone who could advise me.

Before I left for D.C., I made one last attempt to collect sample envelopes from the other auditors around the state—but it still seemed most of them had their heads in the sand about how crucial it was to grease the wheels for mail-in voting, for both the voters and their staffs. They were in denial about how fast it was catching on with voters around the state. They seemed happy to let vote-by-mail grow on its own; none were shuttering polling places to encourage it, like I was.

In D.C., I met a Postal Service official—I can't remember his name—who dropped some pearls of wisdom on how to shrink the whole return package down to size. He also recommended that I meet with Arthur Cowan, our postmaster in Tacoma, to hammer out some ground rules and working conditions before elections rolled around.

I took these new ideas to the envelope company, and we got to work on a new design. I reached out to Mr. Cowan as soon as I returned home and we set up a standing meeting in advance of every election, to work out the kinks. We became true partners in voting by mail.

Soon after my return, the gentleman I'd met with in D.C. gave me a call. He'd been impressed by my knowledge of the issues involved with mass mailings.

"Cathy," he said. "I think you'd be a great fit for our Mailers Technical Advisory Committee, the MTAC. Would you accept an appointment?"

The MTAC is a forum for the Postal Service to share information with, and receive advice from, people who handle mountains of mail. I told him I would love to hop on board—I thought it would be a great way to learn even more about these issues, and maybe throw my two cents in about how to handle mass mailings.

So I was off to D.C. three times a year, to rub elbows with the U.S. Postmaster General and representatives from some of the biggest mailers in the country—Reader's Digest magazine, Publishers Clearing House, and other big shots. I soaked up more about mailing than I'd ever thought possible, and I was getting to know people at the national level who had influence in the field.

My job was complicated, with all sorts of responsibilities,

and so these national outfits were a godsend. At the Election Center's meetings, I picked up priceless tips from election folks from all over the country. As part of MTAC, I was getting the inside scoop on how mailing operations could be more streamlined, economical, and convenient. And as we worked with Griffin and Uarco to make the envelopes and ballots more user-friendly, we took them out for test drives: We visited local civic groups, along with a vote-tallying machine, and let folks try their hand at opening an envelope, filling out a mock ballot, and feeding it into the machine. Then we showed them how their vote was counted. Bit by bit, we were taking the sting out of voting by mail. In time, we whittled that return envelope down to normal size. It cost 32 cents to mail.

I was so happy with the progress we'd made that I decided to try an experiment: For the September 1995 primary, we would vote entirely by mail—a practice the state had just greenlit. Twelve other Washington counties were doing the same thing.

I aimed to prove two things with this experiment: First, that we'd get a lot more folks voting. People were pretty apathetic in these off-year primaries—for the last one, in 1993, only 14 percent of registered voters bothered to cast ballots. I knew we could do much better than that, and that once they saw how easy and secure it was, they'd sign up to be permanent mail-in voters in droves—adding to the more than 70,000 already signed up in Pierce County.

Second, I thought it would save money—about $300,000 by my count; a third of the cost of a normal off-year primary—for the local taxing districts who paid for these elections.

We knew we'd be catching flak from all sides, so we did all we could to prepare everyone, and told them what was coming: We'd be sending out ballots between August 28 and September 2, and voters would have until September 19 to fill them out and postmark them. If they couldn't get over the idea of not leaving their house on Election Day, they could visit one of the drop-off sites around the county. At these sites, a representative from each political party would mark every ballot with the date, time, and their initials before placing them in a secure collection box. Unhoused registered voters could vote at the Tacoma Rescue Mission. We would hire some extra hands to deal with all the folks who wanted to sign up for permanent mail-in voting.

Despite all these preparations and safeguards, as expected, the idea for the experiment came under attack. The editorial cartoons were even more baffling this time. Don Snowden drew a split-panel cartoon in the *Peninsula Gateway* depicting a man mistakenly throwing away his ballot as junk mail—and then later, on September 19, primary Election Day, wondering where his ballot was. Chris Washburn, in the *Pierce County Herald*, drew me with a clipboard, apparently trying to register a man who made his home in one of those blue U.S. Postal Service sidewalk mailboxes. Maybe Washburn had a problem with trying to register homeless voters? Anyway, the guy in the mailbox is complaining that it gets crowded during Christmas and elections, and that maybe the voter pamphlet would be smaller if I kept my name off it.

Cartoon by Chris Washburn

Again: What? It was easy to ignore these criticisms, if that's truly what they were. After all, no sane person could think they raised any issue that needed solving.

I was so fired up about the primary, after I'd mailed out the ballots I told the *News Tribune*: "It will never be the same. We can hardly wait until next week. It's kind of like waiting for a baby to be born."

And that baby came out kicking and screaming: Over 37 percent of registered voters returned their ballots, more than double the 1993 primary. Nearly 22,000 folks signed up to become permanent vote-by-mail voters, bringing the total to 92,000.

But, as I already knew from more than two decades in public service, we couldn't please everyone. Some people were still griping about having to pay return postage. One woman, interviewed by a *News Tribune* reporter, flat-out said: "I will not pay to vote." That seemed like a lot to give up for 32 cents—fortunately, most people weren't that pigheaded.

Our new envelopes were more compact—but some people still found them hard to use. They thought the instructions for returning the ballots were too complicated, and they had to resort to patching up their mistakes with Scotch tape. I told everyone not to sweat it; their ballots would still be counted.

Quite a few ballots were returned to the post office marked "return to sender"—meaning our voter rolls clearly needed updating.

Some voters got their noses out of joint because their ballot arrived before their voter pamphlets. The post office had dropped the ball—but the pamphlet still arrived before the election. I didn't think it was a big deal, but I made sure it wouldn't happen again.

The biggest headache was one we still hadn't resolved, and one still being hashed out by the courts, Secretary of State Munro, and the legislature: how these mail-in ballots should be handled from start to finish. We were playing by the rulebook—but the rulebook was vague and incomplete. Some people were still mad about us opening mail-in ballots and feeding them into the machines before Election Day—even though we weren't counting the votes until after the polls closed. This was why Dale Washam's lawsuit against us had been tossed out.

But this didn't stop him from coming at me from another angle: As we were getting the ballots for September out the door, he filed a petition to recall me from office, accusing me of playing fast and loose with the rules and breaking my oath of office. The petition was a rehash of old charges that had already been dismissed, with a few new ones thrown in—I guess Dale thought I spent too much money traveling to attend official conferences and meetings.

I think he was just trying to harass me. I was too busy to care much about the petition, so I sent it to my lawyer to give it the once-over. But it didn't matter. Less than a month later, before the November election, a judge tossed the petition out on its ear before Dale could even try to get signatures on it. None of his charges were worth the paper they'd been written on.

But I knew he and his pals weren't done with me. They were just getting warmed up.

⁕

In the November general election, we opened the polling places and went back to doing things the old way, but I was still riding high on how well the primary had gone. Voting by mail was more popular than ever. So at the beginning of 1996, I decided to crank it up a notch: I added 121 mail-in precincts to the thirty we already had in Pierce County—in other words, I shuttered 121 polling places, in precincts that had fewer than 200 eligible voters. This was the threshold permissible by law. The press made it seem like we'd gone hog wild—we'd jumped from thirty to 151 mail-only precincts—but it only added about 24,000 mail-only voters to a number that was already north of 100,000 in Pierce County. I also consolidated the county's polling places in densely populated areas, shrinking the total from 228 to 170.

The bellyaching that followed was the same old stuff: Forcing people to vote by mail amounted to an illegal poll tax. Voting by mail wasn't secret. It wasn't secure.

I was tired of listening to it, but it was my job to listen, and to respond to the people's will. So I announced that if more than 200 voters in any of these precincts registered to vote in person, the precinct could switch back.

This was by far the most gung-ho push for vote-by-mail in the state, if not the country, and Republican state legislators clearly wanted to tap the brakes: They introduced a bill to drop the number of voters needed to keep a polling station open down to 100.

Even the loudest critics of our ballot processing had to admit there wasn't a lick of proof that we were up to no good—and nobody had ever credibly accused us of it. One of the Republican legislators who voted for the bill, Mike Carrell, gave an interview before the September primary, saying, "I'm not saying there's any hanky-panky going on. I just think it opens up a can of worms we should not be opening."

I'd already cracked that can wide open, and I invited anyone to come on over to the auditor's office and take a look inside. Quite a few folks took me up on the offer.

It was around this time that I locked horns with a new troublemaker who decided to paint a target on my back. I'll call her Heather. She'd made a name for herself years back as a rabble-rouser who'd fought for term limits and won, and now it seemed like she was itching for a new fight—and that she might be in cahoots with my very own Wile E. Coyote, Dale Washam.

Heather had heard about how we were processing mail-in ballots—because I had been shouting from the rooftops, every which way I could, exactly how we were processing ballots. We were still doing things as they'd been done under the last auditor—only with a much higher profile, now that vote-by-mail was spreading like wildfire. We hadn't changed much—except find a bigger space—since Dale Washam's first lawsuit had been laughed out of court. The rules about when election workers could open mail-in ballots were the same. Verifying and organizing hundreds of thousands of ballots before Election Day, with security tighter than a drum, usually enabled us to tally and announce results within hours of the polls closing. But Heather, and the organization she was affiliated with, had a real bee in their bonnets about it, and wouldn't let it go.

I had nothing to hide and flung our doors wide open to them, and to anyone who wanted to observe what we did.

Meanwhile, Dale Washam was at it again, filing another recall petition, another rehash of old charges with some new ones thrown in. A month later, in March, another judge kicked it out of court before Mr. Washam could try to collect signatures. A few months down the road, Mr. Washam decided to sue Newt Gingrich, Speaker of the U.S. House of Representatives, for plagiarizing his idea for a "Contract with Washington" and turning it into his "Contract with America." Gingrich's lawyer fired back, calling Mr. Washam "a perennially unsuccessful political candidate and litigant." Mr. Washam thought it over, and decided maybe tangling with the Speaker of the House wasn't such a great idea after all.

But he and his new partner in crime, Heather, weren't done trying to drag me to court. She convinced a state Supreme Court justice, just prior to our September 1996 primary, to slap us with a restraining order, preventing us from feeding any ballots into the machines until Election Day. Around the same time, Secretary of State Munro issued "emergency regulations" for handling ballots: Auditors, to keep everything looking squeaky clean, had to cool their heels and wait until after the polls closed to feed ballots into the system. The state Supreme Court would later back him up, and—years later—the legislature would set it in stone. I could see which way the wind was blowing.

So I told my crew to hold off on running ballots through the scanners until after the polls closed—and I did my best to warn everyone that counting votes would now take a few days past Election Day. I didn't have the staff or the equipment to get them tallied and reported on Election Night. The results came out days later.

I scrambled to avoid the same situation for the November general election. I needed more ballot-counting machines—the county only owned two—but they cost $75,000 each, and I didn't have the budget for a new one. I decided to rent a couple, and hire some temp workers to staff them. By now, half the county's registered voters—about 145,000 people—had signed up to be permanent mail-in voters. We were only equipped to count about half that amount by the end of Election Day.

After complaining to the newspapers that I was asking for the moon, Doug Sutherland finally relented and agreed to rent a couple more machines, and approved the hiring of more than a hundred temp workers. It was going to be a busy Election Day for them: Their shifts would begin at five in the morning and end at midnight.

I was completely open with the public about what we were doing, and invited them to watch the entire process, if they wanted. My only request was that they sign in with security and get a visitor's badge. For obvious reasons, we wanted to know who was in the building while votes were being counted.

I guess Heather and one of her sidekicks had other ideas. A few days before the election, they waited for one of the staff to exit a side door to use the restroom, and then ran inside, equipped with a camera to snap pictures of my staff while they processed ballots. A security officer, who was working the over-time shift and guarding the warehouse, confronted them and asked why they weren't wearing visitor's badges. They tried to bulldoze past him and a bit of a scuffle ensued. To this day, I'm not exactly sure what they were hoping to dig up with their sneak attack: Maybe they figured we were up to no good somewhere else in the building, while observers watched us doing things by the book? I still think the whole thing was staged. I think she wanted to make our security people look like the bad guys. I think she wanted people to feel outraged—but she was never very good at explaining what there was to be outraged about.

Just when I thought things couldn't get any nuttier, a bunch of Republican politicians were happy to prove me wrong. They came barging in a few hours later, preening for the cameras and claiming they'd heard we were mishandling ballots. One of these jokers had the gall to tell a reporter he thought the state should take over vote-counting in Pierce County—and to this day, I'm a little pissed that the *News Tribune* printed that, because that same article said these Republicans couldn't find a lick of evidence we were doing anything wrong—but they were still "concerned." About what? They were literally watching our every move.

This little circus act launched another round of courtroom drama: Heather and her sidekick sued the county. The security officer turned the tables and sued them for defamation, a case he won a few years down the road. And Dale Washam—who was now running for Doug Sutherland's county executive seat, and was about to get his clock cleaned again—wrote a letter to the secretary of state, begging him to order us not to open the ballots until Election Day. The secretary of state's office told Mr. Washam to take a hike unless he had some actual proof we were messing with the ballots.

It was all so irritating and exhausting. It felt like I was spending more time putting out fires and fending off these crackpots than actually doing the job folks elected me to do. But I had an idea I thought would make everyone happy—or would at least shut the critics up for a while.

Sometime in 1997, our Director of Public Works, John Trent, came knocking. He knew I often attended NACRC conferences and seminars. He belonged to a similar organization for Public Works directors, and he'd begun the process of climbing the ladder to become its president. The pecking order was the same for his group as it was for NACRC, and for a bunch of other professional outfits: First, you'd throw your hat in the ring for First Vice President, and if all went well, you'd move up to Second Vice President, then Third Vice President, then President. They called it "going through the chairs."

"Cathy," John said. "I notice you go to a lot of NACRC conferences and meetings. Have you ever thought about going through the chairs yourself?"

I hadn't, but it made sense. It would be an achievement not only for me, but for Pierce County. But it also meant more time away and a busier travel schedule, which the county would have to pay for. I knew Doug Sutherland wouldn't be keen on shelling out the funds for that, and under normal circumstances, he would have told Pat Kenny to stiff-arm me. But he couldn't: He'd already approved every expense for John Trent as he went through the chairs, and it would be an obvious case of discrimination if he refused to do the same for me. So I put myself on track to achieve this honor for us in the year 2001.

In the meantime, I got a surprise pat on the back that had nothing to do with my job: Every year, on the first Sunday in June—National Cancer Survivors' Day—all members of the U.S. Congress get to bring one of their constituents, a breast cancer survivor, to the U.S. Capitol Building for a big ceremony of recognition. This year, Rep. Norm Dicks decided to invite me, and sent me a plane ticket. I would stay with him and his wife, Susie, he said.

Norm couldn't meet me at the airport, though, because he was at Vice President Al Gore's birthday party at the Naval Observatory. He sent his assistant, George, who treated me to dinner and then dropped me at Norm's house, where Susie gave me a warm reception. On Sunday, we survivors were wined and dined at a fancy luncheon and ceremony.

It was an incredibly emotional weekend for me. I hadn't really thought about my cancer that much. It was so long ago— twenty-five years, when Ralph and I had gotten sick at about the same time. A lifetime ago. So much in my life had changed. Only one other person at the ceremony had been cancer-free longer than I had. We were both singled out for special recognition.

There was a big social function that night, where I got to meet many other survivors and share stories. For once, it felt like I wasn't being put under a microscope for what I was or wasn't doing at my job. These folks were celebrating me for who I was and what I'd been through. It was two days of feeling really, really special.

On our way home from the event, Susie and I were going to stop for dinner, but the skies opened up and a huge driving rain came down. We wouldn't have been able to make it from the car to the restaurant without getting drenched. So we decided to just go back to their house and have tomato soup and sandwiches. We got home, changed into our jammies, and had just started on our sandwiches when Norm arrived home after attending the hearings about the affair President Clinton had been having with one of his aides, Monica Lewinsky. He brought us up to date. A few months later, the president would be impeached by the House of Representatives. What a crazy time to be in D.C.

◦⁀୬◦

Day by day, more folks were opting to permanently vote by mail. The old print shop was busting at the seams. I started wondering if our tight space, crammed with people handling ballots, looked a little messy, a little unprofessional. It seemed our critics were more concerned with how things looked than they were with what was really going on.

It was obvious we needed more room to process and count ballots than we had in our offices. So I called Doug to give him the heads up: I needed to start scouting out a bigger space. To my surprise, he immediately agreed and told Pat, the budget director, to help me in my search for a building to buy as a ballot-processing center. I think the whole vote-by-mail thing was starting to grow on Doug: I'd saved the county a lot of money in the 1996 elections, and he seemed pleased with that—though he'd rather swallow a toad than admit it to me.

So Pat and I hit the pavement, checking out some of the big buildings around Tacoma, but none of them fit the bill. I was starting to think the best place for us would be in the warehouse where we were already stashing the voting machines. There was plenty of room there, a big open area we could reconfigure to meet our needs, and it was close to the annex. I asked the owner if he'd be willing to sell—no dice, but he was happy to let us keep leasing, and gave us the okay to remodel as we pleased.

Now came the work. There was no roadmap, no blueprint to follow. Oregon, one of the leading states for mail-in voting, had been voting by mail for about five years—it had just held the first all-mail federal primary in November of 1996—so I thought I would take some staff down to see some of their big ballot-processing centers. But we discovered there weren't any, really. Oregon was ahead of the pack, but nobody had yet designed a center specifically for handling mail-in ballots. Like us, they had made do with the space they had on hand. I did notice their specially made drop boxes for the ballots, dolled up to look like little red, white, and blue houses. I fell in love with those, and asked for the plans—and I took them home and hired a carpenter to build and paint several we could place throughout the county.

*One of the original Pierce County
Vote By Mail drop boxes*

Now, for the warehouse. As nobody to date had needed a dedicated ballot processing center, I turned to my former job as a designer. First, I outlined which projects had to be accomplished in this area. Then, I factored in the high security and visibility we would need to work into the layout. Thank goodness we had enough space to accommodate all we needed—efficiency, security, and above all transparency—to soothe the paranoia of our worst conspiracy nuts. We took the machines stored on tables—each with fifty or more square feet of its own—and lined them up on shelves against one wall. Every job had its own dedicated space: an area for checking signatures against the ballots; for repairing or remaking ballots that had been damaged; for the counting machines to do their thing. We built a covered walkway, with windows on both sides, that would give visitors a gander of each step of the process. We figured this was necessary, to keep observers like Heather from poking around and putting their hands on equipment they had no business touching.

Come May, while we were still working on our new Election Center, Dale Washam filed his third recall petition against me. He'd already decided to run against me again in the 1998 general election, so it wasn't hard to figure what he was up to. The charges this time were mostly warmed-over variations of the old ones, but I got a kick out of one of the new ones: Because he couldn't show the secretary of state any evidence that I'd mishandled ballots, he charged that I "intended" to tally them illegally.

You're probably tired of hearing about Dale Washam's recall attempts. Imagine what it was like to deal with them, over and over! Each one looked like it had been cribbed from the one before, using words and phrases that had been rejected by the courts already. Even the *News Tribune* was fed up with him. The paper ran an editorial calling for limits on people's ability to file recall petitions: "Washam," the editors wrote, "appears to be abusing the process to pursue a vendetta against a politician he was unable to defeat at the polls." Couldn't have said it better myself! Less than a month later, a Superior Court judge tossed out the petition.

Nevertheless, he persisted. Two weeks after the filing was rejected, I was hit with another recall petition—by one of Dale Washam's friends, Mark. Dale had helped him write it. The charges in this petition were the same as Dale's—but I think those two guys thought they were pulling off some kind of legal jiu-jitsu: Most of the charges in Dale's petition were tossed because they'd already been tossed by other judges—but since this was the first time Mark was making the allegations, they thought the judge would see this as a clean slate.

Unsurprisingly, the Superior Court judge didn't think changing the name on a petition made its charges any more solid. He tossed it out like yesterday's trash.

While the judges were doing their jobs, we did ours. We painted a huge American flag on one wall. We built a break room and restrooms. We had plenty of room to process the mail-in ballots now—more than 167,000 of them—and we had set up a guided tour for visitors to watch every step of the show, without getting their hands on the ballots.

We'd tried hard to lay out the space so that at least one wall of every room was viewable through the walkway windows, but it just wasn't possible. So for those few spaces that were at least partly out of sight, we set up cameras and displayed video feeds in the walkway. The grand opening was a huge event—it might have been the first facility of its kind in the United States—and election officials from all over the country came to see it.

One person who didn't visit? Heather. She never showed up when she was invited; she preferred the element of surprise. But that didn't stop her from running her mouth to the newspapers about the place she hadn't even laid eyes on.

We didn't have every detail buttoned up yet. It would be a while before we put our new Election Center through its paces in a big general election. But we'd laid the groundwork for our county—heck, for every county in the nation—to make voting by mail as routine as brushing your teeth, secure as Fort Knox, and widely accepted. I know a lot of my critics thought I was moving too fast. But I could see where things were going, and it really felt like we were setting the bar not just for the State of Washington, but for the entire country. And the next few years would prove it: There was no turning back.

CHAPTER 14

The Fabulous Four and The Power of Women in Politics

(1998–2002)

1998 KICKED OFF WITH a bang, with the courts putting my self-proclaimed enemies in their place: A judge finally tossed out Heather's claim that her civil rights had been violated when she broke into the ballot processing center. The newspapers praised the decision, writing that her group had been causing a lot of trouble and a waste of taxpayers' money.

Dale Washam, not to be outdone, had dragged us to court too. There weren't any big county offices up for grabs in the 1997 general election—but God forbid Dale sat one out, right? So he ran for a spot on the Puyallup School Board, and lost, and then sued to have the results overturned, because he didn't like the way we handled ballots. Within weeks, a Superior Court judge tossed his suit for lack of evidence.

But we knew our winning streak wouldn't last forever. This was an election year, and we'd shaken things up in Pierce County—and not everyone loved those changes. I knew I was in for a dogfight in my 1998 reelection campaign, and figured folks were going to have a lot of questions, so I made myself regularly available: I sent out word that every Wednesday, I would be at a specific place to meet with constituents and field any questions they had about voting. I usually took Dave along with me, because he was so good at shooting the breeze, and most often we'd set up at the entrance of supermarkets or neighborhood groceries, where we would meet all sorts of folks. The public loved it, and I felt like I was really turning down the heat on voting by mail.

Meanwhile Dale Washam continued to make a spectacle of himself, trying to get an initiative on the ballot to change how mail-in ballots were processed. It was half-baked, and it went nowhere. But I don't know if getting it passed was really what he was after. He wanted attention for his next big announcement: He was going to be running against me for auditor—again!—this time as an independent. He couldn't run as a Republican, because the Republicans had already made their choice: Rep. Scott Smith, state legislator for Pierce County's rural 2nd district, which stretched east toward Mount Rainier. Mr. Smith was not a fan of voting by mail—he was one of those politicians who wanted to make it harder for people to vote—and he'd adopted a weird strategy, sending out a mailer bragging that he was a dyed-in-the-wool Christian and staunchly pro-life. I wasn't the only one scratching my head, to wonder what the hell that had to do with being Pierce County Auditor, but Smith was also a member of the Insurance Committee, so he had some heavy hitters in his corner. It was going to be a tough fight.

The campaign was chugging along nicely, and we were gradually selling more people on the idea of voting by mail. But then we hit a couple of speed bumps.

It started with John Gamble, who'd managed to stay out of big trouble for a few years, now—but I guess he couldn't keep a lid on it any longer. One day in the summer of '98, he didn't show up to the office. He hadn't called or emailed, which wasn't like him—but we were always so busy that I didn't have time to think about it. I figured I'd get an explanation from him later.

But later that afternoon, I got a call from Dave Viafore, the mayor of Fircrest, a little town west of Tacoma.

"Hi, Cathy," he said. "Do you know where John Gamble is?"

I told Dave I hadn't seen him all day, that he hadn't come into the office.

"Well, he won't be in for a while. He's in our jail."

Seems John had tried to get his phone sex for free this time. He'd harassed a Fircrest woman—his buddy's ex-wife—with a creepy phone call that spooked her enough to call the police, and to move in with her mother for a while.

He made bail on one of my grocery-store Wednesdays, and marched right up to the table where Dave and I were set up.

"Cathy," he said. "Can I talk to you? Alone?"

He must have thought I was still in the dark, because while he admitted to the facts Dave had relayed to me, he added a layer of B.S.: It was just a joke, he said, that had been misinterpreted. He was very sorry.

In its story on the incident, the *News Tribune* printed what John had said in the call. It was clearly no joke. If you'd heard it, it would've curled your hair.

"John," I said, "we're in the middle of a tough campaign. And you might have just cost us the race. You're on paid administrative leave right now. But if we win the election, you're done."

He had no choice but to swallow that bitter pill. The judge didn't think his joke was very funny, either. John was found guilty, slapped with a fine, and ordered to stay away from the woman.

⁓

Not long after the *News Tribune* endorsed me for auditor, the voters of Pierce County got their October surprise. It wasn't dug up by either of my opponents, though: After reading an interview I'd given the newspaper, Heather decided to do some digging around about my college days. I'd told the reporter I'd double-majored in home economics and business administration at the University of Washington. Publicly, I'd never claimed to have graduated from the university, but Heather got it in her head to poke around. Apparently I had, in a deposition for the lawsuit John Gamble had brought down on us, used the word "graduated" when talking about my education—I don't remember saying it, and to this day I couldn't tell you why I used that word, when all I meant to say was that I'd gone to UW.

But oh boy, did Heather make a case of it. She dug up my college transcripts, and kicked up a storm. The *News Tribune* editors yanked their endorsement—but also said they couldn't endorse Smith or Washam: "Both are irrationally opposed to any preparatory handling of early-arriving mail ballots—handling that is perfectly legal, routine in other large counties and necessary to produce timely election results."

The voters agreed with that, at least. I won a second term, without the endorsement. But Heather had finally put a chink in my armor. It stung that the newspaper, and maybe some of its readers, thought I was being untruthful. But the voters had shown they still trusted me, and now I had four years to patch up that damage—and to make voting easier for more of our constituents. And I got to work fast.

Before the new term had even begun, I had to bring in some fresh blood. And these weren't just any old hires. First off, I needed a new deputy—and I was already thinking about who might fill my shoes down the road. I was limited to two terms, and Pierce County was going to get a new auditor in 2002. I racked my brain, going over everyone I knew—and the most capable person I could come up with was my friend Pat McCarthy.

I figured it wouldn't be a tough sell: Pat didn't really like rocking the boat—she liked to stay neutral up there in "Switzerland." She was working for UW's Tacoma campus, and I knew her salary wasn't great, for someone with her talents. I thought maybe I could lure her with the deputy auditor's salary, which was quite a bit higher. So I decided to give it a shot. I phoned her.

"Cathy," she said. "I'm honored. But no way. You're too controversial. You're a pain in the neck. You're always fighting. Why would I want anything to do with that?"

I told Dave about it later that evening, and he suggested we bring Pat's husband, John—who was still serving as a Pierce County judge, and had more of a mind for money than Pat—into the conversation.

We invited them to dinner at a downtown steakhouse, and Dave and I took it slow, asking about the kids—they had four, with two in college—and their jobs, steering things toward my second sales pitch: I reminded Pat of the big difference in what she was making now, at UW-Tacoma, and what she'd make as my deputy. She brushed me off again, telling me she didn't like politics—but I could see the wheels turning in John's head. His eyes lit up.

"Pat," he said. "Why don't you just give it a try?" He and Pat had two more kids to send to college, and I knew that was weighing heavily.

We didn't get an answer that night. But a week later, Pat called to tell me she was on board. I was overjoyed.

But I was also down an assistant: Joan had told me she'd finally decided to retire. She'd become a good friend and one of my most trusted hands, and I was at a loss for how to replace her. A few days after I'd hired Pat, I was chatting in my office with Ken Madsen, the Pierce County Assessor-Treasurer, and told him my dilemma.

"Why don't you ask Keri Rooney from Olympia?" he said.

Keri and I had remained friends ever since she'd replaced me as Senator Ted Bottiger's assistant. After Ted had hung up his hat, she went to work for the governor's office—which is why I'd never imagined Keri would want to work for me. But I knew her well enough to know she would get along with Pat, so I decided to give it a shot. To my surprise, Keri said she was interested in the job. Her son went to school in Tacoma, and she seemed happy to come home, rather than commute to Olympia. I hired her on the spot.

The final piece of the puzzle was the administrative secretary. I promoted a gal from elections, Candy, and I had to admit—this was the best team I'd had yet as auditor. We were the Fabulous Four! I knew we were going to do great things.

And we did. We kicked things off by expanding our outreach programs, with Keri at the helm: We'd finally perfected the return envelopes for mail-in ballots, and we were still sending our folks out to the high schools to show new and soon-to-be voters how to mark their ballots and send them back. We figured out a way to get younger kids involved, too: We launched contests at the elementary schools, with kids competing to design the cover of each voter pamphlet. The kids loved it, and we were all glad to see them engaged in county politics at such an early age.

The program was such a hit that Keri hatched a plan to teach elementary schoolchildren about their county government and elections. She worked closely with teachers, sending out materials and helping them whip their curriculum into shape.

We also rolled out a recognition program for seniors: To every voter sixty-five and older who'd cast their ballot in every past election, we sent an invitation to a luncheon at the Tacoma Dome, the big arena downtown, and recognized each of them with a certificate of appreciation. Some of the folks in assisted living facilities had their families frame their certificate, and soon afterward we had all their names engraved on a plaque we displayed in the Election Center. We invited them to bring their families down to see it, and they came in droves. It was a joyous day, and I think it hammered home the message that voting was an honor and a privilege. Keri had done a great job—good enough to earn an award from the Secretary of State, who recognized our exemplary outreach at two consecutive conferences of the State Auditors Association.

Given how voting by mail was continuing to grow, it was not doable to hire and train up new people for every election. We had about a dozen folks who'd been regulars during the election rushes, staffing the ballot processing center in the old print shop. They worked full-time, but only during elections—three or four times a year—and they came into each election knowing exactly what they were going to do, and how to do it. I knew they would form a great core for the crew I needed to staff the new center during elections.

But boy, did I get some push-back from my staff: Apparently it was one thing to have these temp workers nearby, in the same building, but nobody liked the idea of having a bunch of election staff working on their own at another spot—even if it was just three blocks away.

One of my folks, Mike, said, "Cathy, you can't do that. Those people won't know what the heck they're doing."

You can't do that! I wasn't about to back down—it seemed like such a common-sense solution to me, and I couldn't figure out why they were getting so bent out of shape. They all had well-defined jobs to do in the office with me, and they would need to keep doing those jobs during the elections. We needed a team to staff the Election Center. There were so many mail-in ballots now that it was a real question, in my mind, whether we'd be able to simply stuff prepared ballots into envelopes and get them out to voters on time.

But every time I brought the idea up, my staff shot it down.

At that year's conference for the National Association of State Auditors, Comptrollers and Treasurers (NASACT), Pat tried to gather them all together and talk some sense into them, but the discussion didn't go well. After it was over, my elections supervisor and another staffer came to me in tears. They told me they couldn't swallow the idea of giving that much responsibility to a bunch of temp workers.

There was no two ways about it: I wasn't going to be able to bring in extra hires and organize the Election Center with my staff around. So I extended an olive branch—but it was more than an olive branch, and given how things worked out, I have no regrets.

I sent my entire elections staff off on a three-day retreat to Bremerton, and while they were gone, I brought in the team I'd been assembling and worked out a scheme so they could do their same jobs in a new place. I'd hired two incredibly capable floor managers to oversee the work: Joanne, a friend of mine who'd just left her position at Ernst & Young, and Sam Colorossi, the mayor of Orting, one of Pierce County's smaller towns. Two high-powered and distinguished Pierce County leaders.

When the staff got back from their getaway and found these new people there, they went off like a pack of firecrackers. Some of them told me they were going to quit. I ignored them. I told them to do their jobs. Everything would be fine.

And wouldn't you know, the next election went off so well that my office staff had to eat crow and admit the Election Center team knew their business. Over time, they grew to respect them, even like them. It all worked out.

By now, there were so many mail-in ballots that during general elections, we had to operate two shifts a day to get the ballots verified, sorted, processed, and tallied. This gave us two nuts to crack: First, we still didn't have enough hands on deck to get the job done as quickly as needed. And second, critics of voting by mail weren't getting any quieter.

So once again I hatched a plan to kill two birds with one stone: I reached out to the most trusted groups in our community—the Kiwanis Club, the Rotary Club, the League of Women Voters, church groups, you name it—and asked if they'd send volunteers our way to help get us through the election. We pitched it as a fundraising opportunity: Instead of paying temp workers, we'd make donations to the groups who sent us volunteers.

The people from these groups who came to participate in mail-in ballot processing felt good about what they'd done, and about vote-by-mail in general, and they went out to their communities and spread the word: This was a good thing. Their ballots were secure, they told their members. We were making voting easier for the people of Pierce County. I could feel the wind shifting, just a bit. The tone of our critics felt less often like outrage; more like skepticism. I knew some people would probably never come around. But at least they would tone it down enough to let me do my job.

⤳ℯℬℯ⤲

Except Dale Washam, of course. Everything he'd thrown at me over the past five years had been laughed out of court, but now, thanks to Heather's snooping, he had a new charge to throw at me. In May of 1999, he filed another recall petition, accusing me of fibbing about my college days. Within a few weeks a judge dismissed it, ruling my misstatements weren't sufficient reason for a recall. Mr. Washam would go on to drag this nonsense all the way to the State Supreme Court. In the end, he came up empty-handed again. The whole thing fizzled out within a couple of years.

Meanwhile, we were knocking it out of the park at the

Pierce County Auditor's Office. While we were getting the Election Center set up and ready for the big 2000 general election, the U.S. Post Office gave us a hat-tip for all our work in advancing mail-in voting. They invited me to their annual National Postal Forum in Chicago, and I took Pat and Lori Augino from my elections department along for the ride. Together we accepted the Mailing Excellence Award on behalf of the Pierce County Election Department—an engraved trophy, made of Steuben crystal and shaped like an envelope. The award was a pat on the back for our five-year quest for the perfect ballot mailing package, which had gotten more folks voting and saved them more than $560,000 in postage alone. I was happy to take this award back home and show it to supporters and critics alike, proof positive that our hard work had done so much good.

And we didn't stop there. We added another service to our menu: At a NACRC conference, I heard from several county officials that they were taking on passport services—people in their counties were waiting way too long to be issued their passports, given the backlog in processing. Some county agencies were stepping in to ease the pressure and clear the logjam.

I thought this was a great idea, and I took it to Pat Kenny. It was his job to tell me it was going to cost too much—we would have to shell out a special camera rig for passport photos, it would never really be much of a moneymaker, blah, blah, blah—but Pat had long ago stopped putting up much of a fight. We did it my way. We bought the camera, set up shop, and announced to the public that we'd be offering passport services in June of 2000.

Today, passport services bring in more revenue than any of the other services offered by the Pierce County Auditor.

⌘

The 2000 election was a big one, with neck-and-neck races for both U.S. presidential candidates and for Washington State's two hopefuls for the U.S. Senate, incumbent Slade Gorton and his challenger, Maria Cantwell.

We were lucky not to have punch card ballots, like the poor election workers in Florida, so we didn't have to deal with any of the hanging chads that were giving them such headaches in their recounts. Our Election Center team was also aces at repairing ballots before they went into the machines, so when we did our own recount—a statewide do-over requested by the campaign of Senator Gorton, who was down by less than a point—we didn't have a lick of difference in the before and after tallies. In the end, Maria Cantwell was elected to the Senate—an election voted on by nearly 2.5 million Washingtonians—by about 2,000 votes.

The Bush/Gore election upset a lot of folks—and not just the ones who ended up on the losing side. Under the microscope, the way some precincts handled elections, from keeping voter rolls to processing ballots, looked sloppy and incomplete. Punch-card ballots were lousy, and needed to be done away with. The presidential election was ultimately decided by a few hundred votes in Florida, but nationwide, almost 2 million ballots had been disqualified because they showed either multiple votes or no votes at all when they were run through machines.

So after President Bush took office, Congress formed a National Commission on Election Standards and Reform, to study what had gone wrong and come up with a plan to make voting less troublesome and more secure for Americans. Because I was now the president of NACRC—I had gone through the chairs, serving as First, Second and Third Vice President—I was tapped to be a member of this commission. It meant traveling to Washington, D.C., once a month for a year, but I felt it was my duty. And it was an honor. Congress took our report and turned it into the Help America Vote Act of 2002, which laid down how states should run their elections, established a U.S. Election

Assistance Commission, and coughed up the funds to make it all happen. After President Bush signed it into law, he invited us all to join him at the White House, where we celebrated a job well done.

Back when I first became auditor, I wouldn't have dreamed of skipping town for once-a-month meetings. It wasn't just that the work of the National Commission on Election Standards and Reform was incredibly important. It was also the case that I was in the home stretch of my time as auditor. I'd been stepping back a bit, giving Pat more leadership responsibilities, and coaching her as she stepped into the role.

On paper, the job of NACRC president wasn't all that complicated: The only requirements were to coordinate two conferences a year, and to act as a liaison between county government officials and the U.S. Congress. But when I ascended to the presidency in 2001, I didn't want to do the bare minimum. It was an eventful time to be a county auditor—new recording systems were coming online, and vote-by-mail was gathering steam, all over the country—and there was a lot of work to do.

It had always bugged me that the organization didn't have a newsletter sent out to members, so I worked with Sandy Reedy, who planned and coordinated the association's events, to get one written and distributed. I also hosted the President's Board Retreat, a yearly get-together between the NACRC president and the board of directors. Pat and Keri arranged it all: We flew the board members in, treated them for dinner at my house around the pool, and then caravanned to the town of Ocean Shores, where we holed up at the Quinault Beach Resort and met over three days. It was the first time the President's Board Retreat was held on the West Coast, and the board members were overwhelmed by how pretty the Washington shore was. They talked about it every time we met afterward.

Over our four-year stint, Pat McCarthy had really warmed

to the work of the auditor's office, getting taken in by all the good the auditor could do for the community—as I knew she would. And I knew she'd make a great Pierce County Auditor. Dave and I helped her with her 2002 campaign for the office—though she was so capable, I figured she didn't really need the help. Her opponent? Dale Washam, of course. Pat beat the pants off him, by fifteen points. He sued to have the results overturned. His case was thrown out as garbage.

It was just like old times.

ෙ෨෧

As my term came to a close, my direct involvement with Pierce County elections came to a sudden end. I wrote a guest column for the *News Tribune*, suggesting ways to strengthen our democracy by knocking down more roadblocks to voting. This was really a message in a bottle to the voters, though—I wanted them to demand better from their lawmakers. Pat didn't need much help from me. She excelled at her job, and sailed into a second term. She went on to become Pierce County Executive, and the first woman to serve as Washington State Auditor, elected to her first term in 2016.

Of all my public service roles, being Pierce County Auditor was by far the most mind-bending, hair-pulling—and rewarding. With folks constantly breathing down our necks, slinging mud and dragging us to court, we still managed to pull off some jaw-dropping wins and earned recognition at both the state and national levels. I think most of the criticism during those years wasn't really about the improvements we were making: It was about me, and my style of doing things. I was stubborn, outspoken, controversial—a pain in the neck, like Pat said. And maybe I did push too hard sometimes. I apologized every time I thought I was wrong—but I'll be honest, I didn't think I was wrong very often. Too many things had happened over the years to prove me right.

We'd started with 15,000 mail-in voters, and ended up with nearly all of our 682,000 registered voters getting their ballots in the mail. We'd saved the county a boatload of cash by shuttering all but three polling places. More voters were participating in off-year and special elections. We'd managed to scan and upload all the dusty old paper records into our new recording system, making sure no piece of Pierce County history would ever go up in smoke. The other departments—auto licensing, marriage licensing, passports, the whole lot—were sailing along. I knew I'd left them in good hands.

CHAPTER 15

I Did It My Way, Epilogue

TOWARD THE END OF my last term as auditor, it really started to sink in: These years, among the richest and most rewarding of my life, were about to come to a sudden end. On top of being auditor, I'd been very active in the National Association of Election Officials, and I was now finishing up my NACRC presidency. Now, as 2003 approached, I really didn't want to leave it all behind. I was seventy years old, and felt like I had more to give. But what was I going to do now?

In late 2002, at one of my last Election Center meetings in Washington, D.C., I was talking it over with one of the legislative gals. I told her I didn't know what I was going to do when my term was up.

"Well, Cathy," she said, "I think the choice is obvious. Nobody knows more about voting by mail than you do. The election community needs people like you to help with the mail-in ballots."

On the flight home, I gave it some thought. Maybe she was onto something. Maybe I could connect with election departments around the country and teach them how we did things in Pierce County—and how they might spruce up their own operations. I decided to jump in with both feet and formed my own consulting business: Votes Count, Inc.

I'd been to more trade shows than I could remember, so I

knew just what I needed to get my new business off the ground. I hired a designer to put together a flyer for me. I ordered a boatload of golf balls with "Votes Count, Inc." stamped on them—the boys at those trade shows loved their golf—and fired off notes to every recorder and election official I knew, telling them I was going to be in business after the first of the year—and that I hoped to see them at the Election Center's first conference of the year, down in Florida. I was off to the races.

I didn't have time to mourn the end of my political career: At the first of the year, I set off for the Election Center's Congressional Update Committee Meeting to talk about that year's legislative updates. Pat, Keri, and Lori were there too—but we moved in different circles now as we had different agendas. A few months later, it was time for the Election Center's spring Conference and the debut of my new consultancy business. Dave and I set off for Florida.

Our table was next to one operated by Pitney Bowes, the company that specialized in making postage meters and other mailing equipment. The guys in the booth were showing off a new machine for processing mail-in ballots.

I've never been the patient sort, and I wasn't going to wait for people to come to me. I set out on my own, to introduce both myself and Votes Count to the other vendors in the hall and to any election officials I bumped into along the way. While I was out pressing the flesh, Dave held down the fort with his nose buried in a book.

When I got back to the booth, Dave looked at me sideways and said quietly, "Cathy, I've been listening to those guys next to us, from Pitney Bowes. They've got that machine, but they don't know what the hell they're talking about. You need to go over and explain voting by mail to them."

I told Dave I didn't feel right marching over to our neighbors and telling them they were talking out of their hats. But later in the day, one of their guys came over to pick my brain. His name was Val Guyett—Director of Government Sales for Pitney Bowes—and he was keen to learn what I knew. The conference didn't leave us a lot of time to really dig into the nuts and bolts of their machine, and he told me he really wanted to talk to me in depth, because they were just dipping their toes into the business of mail-in voting. "We see it as the next big thing," he said. "How about me calling you when we get home and we have a cup of coffee?" He happened to live in Olympia.

About a week later, Val rang me up and we agreed to meet at Hawks Prairie, a restaurant about halfway between us. We talked and talked. Val couldn't get enough; he was like a sponge, soaking up everything I'd learned about voting by mail during my ten-year stint. He confessed that he didn't really know how to sell the Pitney Bowes machine, because he'd never quite gotten his head around what election officials did, and how the machine would help them do it. He seemed grateful.

"Hey, by the way," he said. "Do you know Conny McCormack, down in L.A.?" Conny oversaw elections for Los Angeles County—the nation's largest county and a huge market for vendors. I knew Conny well, from our work together on Election Center projects and committees.

"Yeah, I know Conny," I said.

"We've tried and tried," Val said. "But she won't give us the time of day. Won't even give us an appointment. Do you think you could get us in the door?"

"I guess I could try," I said.

I called Conny and she said she'd be glad to see us on Monday—the day after the Super Bowl. And then I called Val and gave him the good news.

"I'll be damned," he said. "Just like that? I'll leave a ticket for you at the airport. See you there."

We landed in Los Angeles on Sunday, and decided to meet

down at the hotel bar to catch some of the big game. Val's associate—some big deal in sales; I can't remember his name—was
there too, and as soon as I sat down, he started firing questions
at me. He didn't ask questions the way Val did, though: He didn't
seem all that interested in my answers. I think he thought he
was the smartest one at the table, and that he was going to prove
it by grilling me. He obviously didn't know what he was talking
about, but it didn't seem to humble him in the least. He was a
real wise guy, and he got on my nerves fast.

The next day, Conny was gracious. She gave us a tour of the
county's election facilities, including the ballot processing center,
and explained how everything worked. She gave us two hours
of her time, and she sat cordially and listened to Val as he went
through his sales pitch. She thanked him for the information,
and we said our goodbyes.

When we got to the elevator, Val's associate, the smart aleck,
looked at me and said, "I didn't see you get a contract signed."

It was beyond irritating. Obviously, he thought this whole
trip was a waste of time. I could tell he resented having to
tag along with us. And I wish he'd stayed home and counted
paper clips.

"Well," I said. "You didn't bring a contract for me to get
signed, did you?"

His face went dark. That shut him up for a while.

I figured I was done with Pitney Bowes after that little
dust-up. But Val called me a few days later and said, "Can you
go with me to the corporate office in New Jersey? I need you
to explain things to the team that's developing our equipment."
It was a smart move. If he was going to sell the new machines,
they had to be able to do what election officials needed: They
had to make issuing and processing ballots more efficient, and
they had to be more secure.

In New Jersey, the bunch of guys Val had rounded up

seemed to be going through the motions. They wanted to cash in on the voting by mail trend with a machine that processed mail-in ballots, but they also seemed to think voting by mail was a flash in the pan, something that would pass. And they didn't seem all that concerned about the kind of machine they were building.

I told them they were wrong. Voting by mail was only going to grow, as voters and election officials realized how much easier and more efficient it was. And it was never going away. If their company wanted to lead the way with a top-of-the-line ballot processing system, it would need to feature both convenience and security. "I don't think you guys really know what you're dealing with," I said.

The room was quiet for a while, and once again I thought I'd put my foot in it. But then the head guy, one of Pitney Bowes's executives in charge of sales, said, "Can you write a business plan for us?"

I'm not sure I knew what a business plan was. I know I'd never written one. I felt the same way I did fifty years earlier, when I'd decided to make drapes and the designer asked if I knew how to make something called a jabot: Nope. But I sure as hell can figure it out.

"Sure," I said. "I can write a business plan."

"Great," he said. "We'll need it by tomorrow."

I hustled back to the hotel room and got cracking: First I learned what a business plan was, and then I put one together. I laid out who Pitney Bowes needed to show their machine to, and where. I listed all the upcoming conferences and events where election officials would be. I worked on it all night—all the way until our eight o'clock meeting, when the big boss looked over the plan. Finally, he slapped it down on the table and said, "That's it. We're doing this. You and Val. Just do whatever you need to do, and I'll have your back."

So Val and I hit the road, showing election officials all over the country Pitney Bowes's new ballot processing technology. The company's engineers took my two cents and built a machine that automatically printed and issued ballots and audited processed ballots when necessary. It was a lot easier to sell a machine with these new features.

Val was the best boss I'd ever had: Voting by mail fascinated him, and he loved learning, both from me and from all the folks he met at conferences and events. He never ran out of questions. It felt like we visited every election official in the country over the next few years, and we were able to convert a good number not only to mail-in voting, but also to Pitney Bowes technology. For a while, it was just the two of us, and it was a blast. But soon Val started butting heads with his sales team. It was the same problem I'd had with them at the start: They were hell-bent on making sales, but they didn't seem to understand, or care about, what they were hawking. And of course, as voting by mail became more widespread, and the processes and technologies matured, customers' needs were changing—and the sales team didn't seem too keen on keeping up with those needs.

Eventually Val couldn't take it anymore, and he left the company. The job wasn't as much fun after that, and I started to see the writing on the wall. At the same time, Dave started feeling poorly. After a knee replacement operation, he started getting infections, and they never seemed to really go away. He went to the hospital a lot, and I felt he needed me to look after him—mostly, I just wanted to be there for him.

I left the company in 2013—it had been a great ride, and we'd done good work that had made a huge difference in the way voting by mail took off in the United States. But like all good things, it had run its course.

ⱻⱻⱻ

I still didn't feel ready to put my feet up just yet. I was itching to do something else, something close to home. I'd always had a soft spot for Bates Technical College, and we were practically neighbors with its South Campus. Back in the 1980s, I'd loved being the go-between for the Tacoma School Board and Bates, and was proud of all we pulled off in that short time: the new programs, the new campus, the increased enrollments. I wanted to be part of all that again, this time as a member of Bates's board of trustees. A recent retirement had left an empty seat that needed filling.

In the years since I'd been liaison, there had been a big change in how Bates—and every vocational/technical college in the state—was run: Instead of the Tacoma School Board calling the shots, Bates was now under the thumb of the Washington State Board for Community and Technical Colleges. It wasn't the superintendent of Tacoma Schools who made appointments to Bates's board—it was the governor of Washington.

I'd been out of state politics for a long time, but I knew the current governor, Jay Inslee, and Dave, through his work with the Teamsters, knew him very well. Dave and I went to a fundraiser down in Olympia, and Dave went right up to him and asked him point-blank to appoint me to the Bates board.

Governor Inslee said yes. It's still amazing to me, how the game of politics works.

I soon got a call from Bates's president, Dr. Ron Langrell, who invited me to meet him for coffee so we could get to know each other. I could tell, from the way he first spoke, that he'd already heard a lot about me, and wasn't all that crazy about having me on his board. But as we talked, he loosened up. He could see I wasn't some fire-breathing dragon lady; I just had a mind of my own. And he seemed to like me, and my opinions—though there wasn't much he could do about them. Things had changed over the years. When Bill Mohler was Bates's president, he'd been happy to let me and his trustees do a little campaigning and drum up interest in the school's programs. Trustees were, by definition, well-regarded and well-connected people who could make things happen.

But Ron explained that this wasn't how they did things anymore. Bates trustees showed up at meetings and events they were invited to. They rubber-stamped the budgets they were handed. They didn't mingle or hobnob with regular folks. Ron didn't say this was how he wanted it; it was just the way things were now, with him getting his marching orders from the state board. I pointed out the obvious: When I was working with Bill Mohler, arranging for his trustees to get out and hype Bates and its programs, enrollment was way up—at capacity, in fact. But now that trustees were cooped up like chickens, stuck in meetings and fundraisers, enrollment at Bates—and at most of the vo-tech colleges in the state—was really hurting. The colleges were under-resourced, struggling financially.

Ron came to trust me, and little by little he gave me some freedom to go out and mix it up with the community. I helped to promote Bates's new Medical Mile Health Science Center in downtown Tacoma, a 70,000 square-foot facility that houses medical and STEM programs. It gives students some real hands-on learning experiences, and provides the community with low-cost health services. It's a beautiful building and a great achievement.

After I'd been on the board a few years, Dave really began to struggle. His infections grew worse, and more frequent, and his body began giving out on him. He was spending more time in the hospital. In May of 2017, he suffered complications from another infection, and never recovered.

I had a really rough time after Dave's death. So often in those early days I would be getting ready to come home after being out with a friend or going to a function, and catch myself think how I couldn't wait to get back and tell Dave about my day. But then I'd remember that he wasn't there. He wasn't sitting in his chair with Lionel, the orange tabby he'd wanted so badly, sleeping on his lap, reading a book, and waiting for me to come home.

We'd begun our relationship more than forty years earlier as best friends, and had stayed best friends that entire time. We shared everything. There was nothing I couldn't talk about with Dave. We were practically stitched together, traveling the country, and the world, in tandem—and loving every minute of it. Our life together ended in the same place, and in the same way, it began: In Tacoma, as best friends.

I still miss Dave terribly.

It would have been nice to have Dave around to help me through the next patch of trouble. Ron Langrell, Bates's president, was a big guy, six-foot-five, and he was a hugger. And some of the gals he hugged weren't too keen on being hugged. It was right around the time folks had started marching around the country with #MeToo signs, to voice their solidarity with other women who'd been sexually harassed, or worse.

I thought Ron's case was a little overblown, and so did another trustee, Tony Anderson. Ron needed to dial back the hugging, and the way he talked to women, and we thought he could do with some retraining and a second chance. We thought he was doing a good job.

But saving Ron's job was like pushing a boulder uphill. The complaints against Ron came just as one of the trustees retired, and Governor Inslee, who knew what was going on, had appointed one of his friends, who worked for him in another State Department, to be the new trustee. It was pretty clear that she'd been sent from Olympia to give Ron the boot, and she seemed to think it was her job to tell the rest of us trustees what to do.

Tony and I could see there was no way we were going to change the other trustees' minds. So Tony introduced a motion to terminate Dr. Langrell "for convenience," which would allow him to seek employment elsewhere, without being branded as damaged goods. It was a unanimous vote.

Given the atmosphere, our next step, hiring a new president, was make-or-break. It needed to be done as quietly and efficiently as possible—but the new trustee had other ideas. She announced that we were going to launch a nationwide search for Bates's next leader.

I thought it was a bad idea. It would take forever, and cost a lot of money, and we already had a great candidate working with us already: Dr. Lin Zhou, our vice president of student success. I managed to convince Tony and another trustee that hiring her would give us a great president and spare us the expense of a nationwide search. The three of us formed a majority vote against the new trustee and her lone ally on the board.

I didn't realize it, but we'd made history: Dr. Lin was Bates's first female president, and the first woman Chinese immigrant to serve as president of a public two-year college in Washington State.

Prior to becoming the president, one of the programs Dr. Lin championed at Bates was an exchange program for higher education officials. Tony and I were invited to accompany her to China, where we visited three different schools and walked a bit on the Great Wall. What an experience!

But Dr. Lin's hiring didn't change the fact that college trustees, now that the state was calling the shots, were supposed to be seen and not heard. The new trustee had been sent from Olympia to hammer that home: Trustees were not cheerleaders. They belonged in the board room, not out pressing the flesh.

Tony and I went out and did it anyway—and on his own, Tony managed to shake loose some big money from donors to the Bates Technical College Foundation.

After the turmoil with Ron was put to bed, the board's atmosphere was still very toxic. At the next meeting, to my surprise, Tony tendered his resignation.

I couldn't believe the direction Bates was headed. After Tony was gone, the new trustee seemed to be on a crusade to strip the trustees of any outside activities. Yet enrollment was way, way down. And Bates had so much to offer. How did they think they were going to bring in new students? Most of the trustees had been businesspeople. They knew it took money to make money.

I felt stuck. Frustrated. And—maybe for the first time in my life—tired of fighting. So I resigned.

But I wasn't done sharing my opinion. I addressed my resignation letter directly to Governor Inslee, and I told him the state's approach to running colleges like Bates was completely backwards: Bates trustees were more than just figureheads. They were community leaders, perfect spokespeople and influencers. Under Bill Mohler, Bates's trustees went out into the neighborhoods and spread the word about what Bates had to offer, letting parents and grandparents know that their young ones, who may not be doing particularly well in high school, had a place to go where they could learn new skills and earn good-paying jobs. The trustees were ambassadors then, not just stuffed shirts who warmed seats at meetings. They knew something today's boards—and the state board who appointed them—seem to have forgotten: Colleges are for students. And the more students a college has, the better it is for everyone.

Governor Inslee—wouldn't you know it!—never answered my letter. But a few weeks later, at a community event, I spotted one of his lackeys and I marched right up to him, aiming to ask if the governor had received it. He saw me coming—I could see his eyes darting around like a cornered rabbit, looking for an escape route, but I got to him just before he could bolt, and I looked him in the eye.

He only managed to look at me for a split second.

"Hi, Cathy," he said. But he was already slinking away, melting sideways into the crowd.

✎✐✎

He wouldn't be the last Big Boy I'd had the opportunity to shut up. I guess he and Governor Inslee didn't like the way I did things. But who had, over all the years of my career? I don't care that some folks didn't like my style. I care that people—from Olympia, Washington, to Washington, D.C.—have recognized and appreciated the work I've done for the people I've served.

When I look back on my life and career, there are three achievements I'm especially proud of: First, that I survived the long illness and death of my first husband, Ralph, with my home and family intact. Honestly, I've never been more scared than I was after Ralph took sick. I could have taken the easy way out. I was grateful to Ralph's father for offering to pay off my mortgage. It was very generous, but I couldn't take it. It wasn't my way. I knew I wouldn't be able to live with myself if I didn't figure things out on my own. And I did.

Second, spearheading efforts that transformed how people in Washington State engage with democracy. Establishing voting by mail wasn't just a convenience; it was about making elections more accessible for everyone, ensuring that no one's voice was silenced because they couldn't make it to a polling place. Creating the voters' pamphlet gave people the tools to make informed choices, empowering them to take ownership of their role in shaping their communities. Those were battles worth fighting, and every ballot cast and every informed vote feels like a personal victory.

Third: I mostly stayed ahead of the Big Boys and their old order, their way of doing things and taking care of each other—setting themselves up in their posh little washroom/cigar lounge, for example—while they discouraged women at every turn, directing us to the public restrooms down the hall. Whenever I came up with a different—and, frankly, much better—way of doing things, they loved to say "You can't do that."

I never spoke the words, but I showed them, again and again: *Yes, I can.* I found my way over, around—and sometimes right through—the obstacles they put in my way, their petty backroom maneuvers and their lawsuits and their smear campaigns.

And I think my results speak for themselves. I never wanted to do things the way they'd always been done. I wanted to do them the way they *should* be done. And as the song (kind of) goes: Sometimes I bit off more than I could chew, but when there was doubt, I ate it up and spit it out. I stood tall, and I did it my way.

My life is quieter now, without the work and without Dave. But it's a good kind of quiet, filled with the hum of life that keeps going. My kids, my grandkids, and now even my great-grandkids fill this home with laughter and purpose. They take care of the big dinners and pool days. I watch them set the table, cook meals, and teach their young ones how to swim. They don't need my guidance anymore—they're capable, thoughtful, and strong. I see it in their every action: the way they rise to challenges, the way they show up for each other, and the way they refuse to back down.

I taught them well, yes—but the truth is, they've taught me something, too. As I sit back and take it all in, I realize: What we build in this life isn't just about getting by and getting things done. It's about leaving a mark—on people, on hearts, and on futures we might never see. And in them, I see my greatest work, my deepest legacy.

They are my proof that this world is brighter because we lived, because we dared, because we fought, and because we loved. And for that, I am endlessly grateful.

Acknowledgments

This book was a dream that lingered in my heart for many years, a project I talked about often but never quite got to. Putting it all down on paper was a sweet realization that I truly did live my life my way. I'm so grateful to have had the chance to finish it before leaving this world.

First and foremost, I dedicate this book to my sons, Joe and Rod. You were so strong during your father's illness, shouldering burdens no child should have to bear. I'm sorry that life wasn't what we hoped it would be. Your dad couldn't be there to teach and guide you through life the way a father should, and I had to be away so much just to keep us afloat. But through it all, you never complained. You took the hard times in stride, and for that, I am forever grateful. I love you both, so much.

Secondly, to the people who made this book happen. My granddaughter, Justine, who pushed me to write the story, made sure my voice came through the pages, and really guided this book from a dream in my head to a hard copy in my hands. Breanna, for helping me to navigate the computer and print the pages big enough for me to read it. Tony and Linda, for helping me proofread it when my eyes couldn't do any more. Without all of you, this book wouldn't have made it this far.

To the rest of my family—my stepchildren, grandchildren and great-grandchildren—you are my joy and my legacy. Watching you grow, thrive, and carry forward the values we hold dear has been the greatest blessing of my life.

A special thank-you goes to everyone—friends, colleagues, family—who believed in my vision and supported the causes that shaped my journey. From advocating for families to transforming how people engage with democracy, this book is as much about the collective work as it is about my story.

Finally, to the readers—thank you for picking up this book and taking the time to hear my story. I hope it inspires you to tackle your own challenges, stand up for what you believe in, and create something lasting and meaningful in your own lives.

I have truly been blessed in this life.

With love and gratitude,
Cathy Pearsall-Stipek

About the Author

Cathy Pearsall-Stipek, born on April 18, 1932, is a lifelong Tacoma, Washington resident and seasoned public servant with a distinguished career in local and state government as well as a small business owner. She attended the University of Washington and started her journey into politics as a member of the local preschool's Parent Teacher Association. She rose through the ranks of the PTA and went on to serve as Representative for the 29th District in the Washington House of Representatives (1977-1979), member of the Tacoma School Board (1983-1989) and the Pierce County Council (1989-1993), Pierce County Auditor (1993-2002), and Governor-appointed member of the Bates Technical College Board of Trustees (2015-2019). She was president of Votes Count, Inc., a consulting and training business focused on improving vote by mail systems. She is a dedicated mother, step-mother, grandmother and great-grandmother.

www.ingramcontent.com/pod-product-compliance
Lightning Source LLC
Chambersburg PA
CBHW051613120626
46551CB00014B/1776